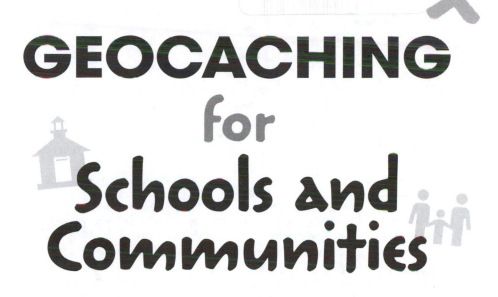

GEOCACHING
for
Schools and Communities

J. Kevin Taylor
DuAnn Kremer
Katherine Pebworth
Peter Werner

Human Kinetics

Library of Congress Cataloging-in-Publication Data

Taylor, J. Kevin, 1965-
  Geocaching for schools and communities / J. Kevin Taylor ... [et al.].
    p. cm.
  Includes bibliographical references.
  ISBN-13: 978-0-7360-8331-7 (soft cover)
  ISBN-10: 0-7360-8331-6 (soft cover)
  1. Geocaching (Game)--Study and teaching. I. Title.
  GV1202.G46T39 2010
  796.1'4--dc22
                                        2010010170
ISBN-10: 0-7360-8331-6
ISBN-13: 978-0-7360-8331-7

The Web addresses cited in this text were current as of June 2010, unless otherwise noted.

Acquisitions Editor: Gayle Kassing, PhD; **Developmental Editor:** Ray Vallese; **Assistant Editors:** Derek Campbell and Elizabeth Evans; **Copyeditor:** Patrick Connolly; **Permission Manager:** Dalene Reeder; **Graphic Designer:** Bob Reuther; **Graphic Artist:** Angela K. Snyder; **Cover Designer:** Keith Blomberg; **Photographer (cover):** Neil Bernstein; **Photographer (interior):** Photos courtesy of the following, unless otherwise noted: J. Kevin Taylor (chapters 1, 3, and 8, and photo on p. 89); DuAnn Kremer (chapter 5, and photo on p. 21); Katherine Pebworth (chapters 2 and 4, and photo on p. 15); Peter Werner (photos on pp. 19, 35, and 41). Photo on p. 4 by Jack Phelan; photo on p. 5 by Lauren Hastings; photo on p. 83 by Neil Bernstein; photo on p. 116 by Mary Werner; **Photo Asset Manager:** Laura Fitch; **Visual Production Assistant:** Joyce Brumfield; **Photo Production Manager:** Jason Allen; **Art Manager:** Kelly Hendren; **Associate Art Manager:** Alan L. Wilborn; **Illustrator:** TwoJay!; **Printer:** Versa Press

Printed in the United States of America

10   9   8   7   6   5   4   3   2   1

The paper in this book is certified under a sustainable forestry program.

Human Kinetics
Web site: www.HumanKinetics.com

United States: Human Kinetics
P.O. Box 5076
Champaign, IL 61825-5076
800-747-4457
e-mail: humank@hkusa.com

Canada: Human Kinetics
475 Devonshire Road Unit 100
Windsor, ON N8Y 2L5
800-465-7301 (in Canada only)
e-mail: info@hkcanada.com

Europe: Human Kinetics
107 Bradford Road
Stanningley
Leeds LS28 6AT, United Kingdom
+44 (0) 113 255 5665
e-mail: hk@hkeurope.com

Australia: Human Kinetics
57A Price Avenue
Lower Mitcham, South Australia 5062
08 8372 0999
e-mail: info@hkaustralia.com

New Zealand: Human Kinetics
P.O. Box 80
Torrens Park, South Australia 5062
0800 222 062
e-mail: info@hknewzealand.com

E4823

CONTENTS

LEARNING EXPERIENCES FINDER

(continued)

Learning Experiences Finder *(continued)*

Discipline	Name	Skill level	Page
Science	Rock This	Beginning	113
Science	The Shinbone's Connected to What?	Advanced	174
Science	Sunrise, Sunset	Beginning	130
Social studies (geography)	Coordinate This!	Advanced	175
Social studies (geography)	Google Earth	Beginning	132
Social studies (geography)	How Many Ways Can I Get There?	Beginning	132
Social studies (geography)	Nowhere, Everywhere	Beginning	132
Social studies (geography)	Rocking on the Road	Beginning	132
Social studies (geography)	State of the Union	Advanced	168
Social studies (geography)	Where in the World?	Beginning	122
Social studies (geography)	Where's Who?	Advanced	175
Social studies (history)	All Around Town	Beginning	133
Social studies (history)	Did You Know?	Beginning	133
Social studies (history)	I Didn't Know That!	Beginning	119
Social studies (history)	I Remember When . . .	Advanced	175
Social studies (history)	Marking My Way	Beginning	133
Social studies (history)	Westward Ho!	Advanced	161
Social studies (history)	What's Happening?	Advanced	174

PREFACE

In May of 2000, President Clinton authorized the use of the Global Positioning System (GPS) satellite system by the general public. Previously, the system had been for military use only, but it was seen as having great potential for civilian applications, along with great commercial possibilities. Being a person who believes in keeping up with new technological development, I soon purchased a GPS receiver and primarily used it for marking good fishing sites and for traveling. It came in handy for route selection and for finding restaurants, accommodations, attractions, and gas stations.

Early in 2001, my children and their husbands informed me of a new sport called geocaching. I was intrigued and went online to find out all about it. I located a listing for a cache in Columbia, South Carolina, near the river walk. I marked the waypoints and went on a hunt with family and friends. Much to our dismay, we were not able to find the cache because some muggles had found it and destroyed the site. (In the world of geocaching, the term *muggle* is used to identify a person who doesn't participate in the sport.) However, I was hooked by the excitement of the hunt for a hidden treasure.

At the national AAHPERD convention in Philadelphia in 2003, I took Kevin Taylor—a former graduate student, fellow adventurer, and colleague—on a geocache hunt for the world's largest cookie factory (Girl Scout Cookies). We found it and then started thinking about the possibility of sharing ideas about this activity with fellow physical education teachers and recreators. In the meantime, I introduced Katherine Pebworth, a graduate student in pedagogy at the University of South Carolina, to geocaching. She quickly became enthused and began helping me teach geocaching to undergraduate students at USC. In the spring of 2003, the three of us wrote a proposal to present two sessions on geocaching at the national AAHPERD convention in New Orleans. One session was to teach those in attendance about the new sport of geocaching. The second session was to go out into the city of New Orleans and find some geocaches. Both proposals were accepted.

During the same period, DuAnn Kremer, an associate professor of exercise physiology at Lander University (Greenwood, South Carolina) and a pedagogy colleague from the same institution, conducted a session on geocaching at the South Carolina AAHPERD convention in the fall of

2003. I attended the session and was impressed with her knowledge and enthusiasm. Eventually, I asked DuAnn to join our group in presenting sessions on geocaching in New Orleans. She accepted and thus our group of four was formed.

Each of us has moved on with our careers. Kevin Taylor moved from the University of Northern Colorado to Cal Poly at San Luis Obispo where he conducts the pedagogy program and also teaches adapted physical activity. DuAnn Kremer moved from Lander University to Lynchburg College where she teaches exercise physiology. Katherine Pebworth graduated from the University of South Carolina and is currently at Lincoln Memorial University where she is in charge of the pedagogy program. I retired from the University of South Carolina and moved to the mountains of North Carolina where I continue to be active professionally by serving as a visiting professor, consultant, and writer. Yet all of us have one thing in common—geocaching.

Over the years, we have conducted numerous sessions on geocaching. Either individually, in pairs, or as a whole group, we have conducted sessions at several state conventions, district conventions, and regional conventions as well as at five national AAHPERD conventions from 2003 to 2008. We have also written journal articles on geocaching and information about geocaching that appears in two books—*Seminar in Physical Education* (2007) and *Interdisciplinary Elementary Physical Education* (2009).

We all share a passion for geocaching. Collectively, we have logged over 1,000 caches representing many states and at least six countries. Caching has allowed us to develop new friendships, to share our zeal for adventure with others, to learn information about people and places we have visited, and to lead active lifestyles. The benefits we derived from geocaching led us to the thought of writing a book about geocaching. But what would we write about? Several trade books on how to hide and seek caches and how to use GPS units have already emerged. We settled on the fact that we are all educators and that our backgrounds in health, physical education, and recreation would allow us to make a unique contribution. That contribution would focus on how geocaching can be used to enhance the school curriculum and promote active, healthy lifestyles from childhood through older adulthood.

Geocaching for Schools and Communities raises awareness of the potential benefits that geocaching can provide when included in physical education and physical activity programs. The book introduces public school teachers to the potential that geocaching has to offer for instructional content, including the potential for cross-curricular integration. To help readers apply the content presented, throughout the book you will find tales from many of the trails that the authors have traversed over their years of geocaching. These "Trail Tales" are interesting stories that illustrate some of the ideas and concepts covered in the text. These stories may also stimulate your imagination and creative thinking as you design your own geocache lessons, sessions, and programs. Careful attention has been paid to selecting real-world examples that are valuable to professionals in all of the diverse settings where geocaching might be used.

The first four chapters of *Geocaching for Schools and Communities* make up part I. This part of the book introduces the basics of geocaching. Part II, which includes the last four chapters, is about implementing the use of geocaching in schools and communities through an integrated approach to curriculum and leading active, healthy lifestyles.

Chapter 1 introduces geocaching and provides a definition as well as a history of this activity. The chapter also identifies potential participants and includes a discussion of the values and benefits of geocaching. Chapter 2 covers the equipment needed for geocaching and some other common applications of technology that can be used in geocaching, such as route guidance systems. Some teachers may be prevented from introducing their students to geocaching because of the expense of GPS units, so chapter 3 explores ways to introduce and teach the principles of geocaching using map and compass work. Chapter 4 explains the different types of caches, how they are typically set, and which type would be most appropriate for use in a variety of educational contexts.

Chapter 5 focuses on the various ways that geocaching can be used to entice people into being more physically active. Geocaching involves being physically active and hence provides physical educators and recreation leaders with another way to motivate people into increasing their levels of physical activity. Chapters 6 and 7 introduce you to the wealth of possibilities that exist for incorporating content from all aspects of the school curriculum into physical education through the activity of geocaching. These chapters provide lesson plans for how you can incorporate geocaching into the curriculum. Two lesson plans are provided from each of the following areas at both the elementary and secondary levels: language arts, mathematics, science, and social studies. Additional ideas for lesson plans in language arts, mathematics, science, and social studies are also included. Chapter 8 helps people who are inspired by the content of this book to take the first brave step toward implementation of a program. Geocaching can be expensive because of the need to purchase GPS devices. This chapter provides suggestions for raising the funds needed for buying a set of GPS devices. It also provides ideas on how geocaching can be used outside the school setting in more recreation-oriented programs.

This book is for public school teachers and university professors who are looking to train their students in the use of geocaching. The book is also for practicing health and physical education teachers, physical activity specialists, and youth and community recreation leaders. The book will appeal to people with a broad range of backgrounds and experience. People who are new to geocaching will get a thorough introduction, including the history and development of the activity. They will learn how the many forms of geocaching evolved. People with some experience in geocaching will receive materials that will help them apply their knowledge in an instructional setting. This book is practitioner oriented. It contains ideas and suggestions for practical application. Examples are provided along with lessons learned from the authors' accumulated experiences.

The motto of geocaching is "The sport where you are the search engine." We hope you will learn to share the joy of discovering the hidden treasures out there in the world. Spread the word. Get involved. Don't be a muggle anymore!

Peter Werner

ACKNOWLEDGMENTS

Writing a book requires help and support from many people. We, the authors, thank the many participants in the workshops we have conducted. We thank them for questioning our ideas and inspiring new ways to view things and an unending desire to try new technology in different ways. We thank John Howell from Garmin and Martha Garcia from Magellan for providing GPS units from their respective companies for use in our workshops. In addition, the editorial staff at Human Kinetics has been most helpful in their dealings with us during the proposal and manuscript preparation phases of this publication. For many years, Scott Wikgren has provided us with encouragement for innovative ideas regarding the use of technology in school and recreational or community settings. Gayle Kassing and Ray Vallese have supported our efforts throughout the proposal and writing process. Thanks also go to the photographers and illustrators whose work brings clarity and excitement to many of our examples and learning experiences.

Finally, we are indebted to our extended families for supporting us through our caching and writing efforts. These people include mothers and fathers, children, grandchildren, in-laws, special friends, and, yes, even pets. We appreciate their kindness, wisdom, and enduring patience. We also appreciate their sense of adventure that has been brought out through an ever-expanding world of geocaching.

All About Geocaching

Part I provides an introduction to geocaching and the use of GPS units. This part of the book is about the history, the nuts and bolts, and the technical aspects of geocaching. Chapter 1 provides an introduction to geocaching, including an explanation of geocaching and a description of caching terminology. The chapter then describes the history of geocaching. From an early history of letterboxing in Victorian England to the use of Global Positioning Systems (GPS), geocaching has rapidly expanded in the years since May of 2000 to a worldwide interest. Chapter 1 also includes a discussion of the people who are attracted to geocaching. Geocaching is a great activity for individuals, parents, children, families, and groups or clubs. The values and benefits of geocaching are also covered in this chapter, focusing on the areas of educational, ecological, physical, social, and family outcomes.

Chapter 2 is all about high-tech geocaching. It includes a discussion of GPS units and the basic features of a GPS receiver. You'll also learn about satellites and the triangulation necessary for locating latitude and longitude coordinates. The use of a computer and the Internet for geocaching is also discussed.

Chapter 3 describes low-tech alternatives that can be used with participants who are too young for high-tech geocaching. These alternatives can also be used by people who want to try out geocaching before investing in a GPS unit. Map and compass skills are discussed in this chapter, along with activities such as letterboxing and urban and landmark orienteering.

Part I finishes with the basics of caching in chapter 4. The chapter starts with a definition of a cache. It then describes items commonly placed in a cache and proper geocaching etiquette. The various types of caches are discussed, and the chapter provides a step-by-step guide to finding and logging a cache.

chapter 1

INTRODUCTION TO GEOCACHING

ooking for things can be fun. That's why hide-and-seek has been an enduring love among children for generations. Childhood fantasies about treasure hunting are driven by the fun of looking for things that other people have lost or tried to hide; treasure hunting is full of adventure, thrills, and challenges. Geocaching is a modern-day high-tech means of looking for treasure in the form of inexpensive trinkets that others have hidden. It is filled with a sense of adventure and challenge but is also a safe activity that people of all ages and abilities can participate in together. Geocaching is a relatively new activity that started in 2000 when then-President Clinton removed the selective availability restrictions on the Global Positioning System (GPS). Removing the selective availability restrictions made the GPS system available and feasible for use by the general public. Before the removal of these restrictions, GPS satellites could only be used with any accuracy by the military.

Geocaching Explained

A **geocache**, pronounced "geo-cash," is a hidden store of trinkets. The word *geocache* comes from *geo,* meaning "of the earth," and *cache,* which is French for hiding place or hidden store. Simply stated, geocaching involves someone hiding a box of trinkets and posting the coordinates of the box's location on the Internet; other people reference the coordinates and then

✘ Children love hide-and-seek because looking for things is fun. Geocaching follows the same principle but with a high-tech twist.

go hunting for the trinkets. People who go geocaching are called **geocachers** (often abbreviated to *cachers*). If you want to go geocaching, you look up the coordinates of a cache, plug them into your GPS unit, and try to find the cache. A cache is normally well hidden so that people who are not actually looking for it don't find it by mistake; therefore, along with the coordinates, the person who hid the cache will usually post a short clue to help people locate the cache once they are within a few feet of the location.

So, you track down the location using your GPS and the posted coordinates, you solve the clue that was posted, and you find the cache. Now what? At a traditional geocache, most geocachers like to swap a trinket—that is, they take something from the cache and leave something in its place. Trinkets can be any small item worth no more than $2. Some creative cachers leave the same trinket every time, and this becomes a calling card of sorts. After finding a cache, most geocachers will log their cache online. They will also track the number of caches they have found. You don't have to log your cache if you prefer not to; some dedicated geocachers simply enjoy the thrill of hunting for a cache. Those who do log their find also sometimes leave comments for the person who set the cache. Geocachers may leave comments to thank the person for setting the cache, to compliment the person on a well-hidden cache, or to report any problems with the cache. An example of a reported problem might be that the cache wasn't properly hidden after the last find. When reporting this problem, the geocacher may include a request for future geocachers to be careful in rehiding the cache more thoroughly. More details on the intricacies of geocaching are covered throughout the book.

✖ A traditional geocache contains trinkets that geocachers trade.

Although more than one Web site is available for looking up and logging a geocache, the most popular site by far is www.geocaching.com. To use the geocaching.com Web site, you set up an account with a user name and password of your choice. A basic account is free and gives you everything needed to start caching. Frequent reference will be made to this Web site as we explore the many intricacies and complexities that have been added to the basic concept of geocaching. Throughout this text, any further mention of logging a cache or looking up a cache on the Internet refers to the geocaching.com Web site unless stated otherwise.

History of Geocaching

Geocaching is dependent on using a **Global Positioning System (GPS)**, so geocaching really began with the opening of GPS satellites to the general public in 2000. Before the year 2000, GPS signals were available but were intentionally degraded through a process known as **selective availability (SA)**, which had been in place to restrict the accurate use of GPS to the U.S. military. As the accuracy of GPS continued to increase, scientists and policy makers began to realize the potential benefits of this technology for civilian use in addition to military applications. With potential civilian applications in mind—along with the huge commercial possibilities that would be available with GPS—U.S. President Bill Clinton announced in 1996 that selective availability would end in 2000. He also announced that an Interagency GPS Executive Board would be created to oversee the use of GPS technology in the United States. The Interagency GPS Executive Board was superseded in 2004 with the creation of the National Executive Committee for Space-Based Positioning, Navigation, and Timing.

Since the end of SA, the use of GPS technology has become remarkably commonplace. This technology is being used for everything from turn-by-turn directions in a car to keeping track of pets. A GPS unit is a very high-tech compass that takes bearings to establish its position in relation to a number of GPS satellites before calculating (through a process of triangulation) where in the world it is located. The calculations involved in determining precise

TRAIL TALE

Kevin

Geocachers have always been concerned with minimizing the impact of geocaching on the environment and cleaning up areas where people like to geocache. I carefully explained this to my two sons before taking them out to find their first geocache. Later, I was quite impressed when my oldest son, Christopher, chastised me for treading on some weeds around the cache site! Now, after finding a cache, we always discuss the relative merits of the cache in terms of how easy it is to find without damaging the environment around the site.

locations around the globe use the **World Geodetic System (WGS84)**, established in 1984. Although WGS84 is largely accepted to be the current standard, you may come across maps that still use the preceding system known as NAD27 (from North American Datum 1927). The number of satellites used by GPS technology has risen steadily since its inception; as of December 2009, the U.S. government listed 30 satellites in use for GPS technology.

According to geocaching.com, the very first cache was placed by Dave Ulmer on May 3, 2000. Dave called it the Great American GPS Stash Hunt. Apparently, Dave was eager to test the accuracy of the new GPS technology, so he put a black bucket in the woods near his Beaver Creek, Oregon, home and posted the coordinates to an Internet listserv of a GPS user group. In the original posting, Dave invited readers to find the stash using GPS, and he indicated that they should "take some stuff, leave some stuff." Within days, avid GPS adventurers shared their experiences of locating the stash, signing the logbook, and discovering the prize items contained in the stash (videos, books, software, and a slingshot). Within a few more days, other readers began to hide their own stashes and share the coordinates.

As with many Internet-based phenomena, the concept started to spread more quickly than anyone would have imagined. Mike Teague was the first person to find the Great American GPS Stash, and within a month, Teague was gathering coordinates from online posts around the world. In July of 2000, a Web developer named Jeremy Irish discovered Teague's site, and after quickly finding his first stash, he began work on his own Web site dedicated to the hobby. At this point, the activity was still most widely referred to as GPS stash hunt, but Irish adopted the term *geocaching*. With Mike Teague's input, Irish launched geocaching.com on September 2, 2000.

A more detailed history of how geocaching began can be found on the current geocaching.com Web site, but needless to say, the growth rate of geocaching was quite remarkable. When the Web site was first launched, there were 75 known caches in the world. According to an online forum hosted by the geocaching.com Web site, the number of registered caches worldwide grew from 150,000 to 550,000 between June 2004 and June 2007. In May of 2010, 10 years after the Web site's initial launch, the number of caches worldwide had surpassed 1 million.

Cachers and Muggles

Initially, geocaching had great appeal to those with GPS systems and those who love playing with technology, but the appeal of geocaching has quickly broadened. People in all walks of life—and people of all ages and all levels of ability—now embrace geocaching as a means of exploring new (and old) places. Geocaching is high-tech hide-and-seek using trinkets and treasure rather than people. Anyone who loves a good scavenger hunt is likely to become an instant convert once he or she tries geocaching. This book introduces ideas for use in educational settings, but it also provides a nuts-and-bolts approach for anyone who is new to the activity. This approach can help a person quickly transition from muggle to cacher extraordinaire.

Groups of people who share an interest in any endeavor often develop their own lexicon based on their chosen interest, and geocachers are no different. As part of the lexicon of geocaching, cachers refer to nongeocachers as **muggles**, a term borrowed from the Harry Potter novels written by J.K. Rowling. These novels are about a parallel world of witches and wizards who refer to nonmagical people as muggles. In the geocaching world, a muggle is someone who hasn't heard of geocaching or hasn't been caching before.

Curious muggles sometimes find a cache after seeing someone discover it. These muggles often don't put the cache back in the right spot, either because they don't know any better or because they don't care. As a result, the cache is more apt to become lost or stolen. Caches sometimes go missing entirely, raising the possibility that uncaring muggles have taken them. A cache placed in a well-populated or busy spot will often carry a warning that urges people to beware of the muggles, meaning simply that people should be careful not to give away the location of the cache while they are finding it. This is an important piece of geocaching etiquette (a more detailed discussion of caching etiquette and lexicon can be found in chapter 4).

Forerunners of Geocaching

Long before anyone had conceived of geocaching, similar activities existed, many of which are still popular today and can be seen as forerunners to what we now call geocaching. These activities include letterboxing, orienteering, and rogaining.

Letterboxing Other than a basic scavenger hunt, the earliest recorded activity that we have found to bear a resemblance to geocaching comes from Dartmoor in England, where **letterboxing** has been going strong since Victorian times. The activity of letterboxing apparently began around 1854; this is when a guide named James Perrot placed a bottle in a bank near Cranmere Pool and had walkers (for whom he acted as a guide) visit the spot and deposit their calling cards. The spot, which at the time posed quite a challenging hike, soon became a popular destination for the more hardy tourists. A tin box had replaced the original bottle by 1888, presumably to allow more room for callers to leave their cards.

By 1905, the custom of leaving one's calling card was replaced by the process of signing a visitor's book, a practice that was in turn replaced by a rubber stamp and ink pad. Eventually, the custom evolved to the practice of leaving a postcard addressed to one's self or to a friend; subsequent visitors would then collect the card and mail it from their hometowns. The enduring popularity of letterboxing led to the local newspaper—*The Western*

Morning News—taking over the site in 1937. At that point, the newspaper covered the cost of erecting a granite box to be the receptacle for cards. Some current estimates claim that there are now upward of a thousand boxes on Dartmoor, most of them well hidden from the casual passerby, just like a geocache.

Dartmoor letterboxes contain clues that will lead you to other letterbox sites and containers. Modern-day letterboxes, much like geocaches, are often old ammunition boxes or waterproof plastic containers. Some of Dartmoor's more historic pubs act as starting points for letterboxers; alternatively, the Museum of Dartmoor Life in Okehampton would be a good place to begin. For those who are unable to travel to Dartmoor, letterboxes can also be found around the globe. A growing number of boxes can be found in North America. These are listed on the Letterboxing North America Web site (www.letterboxing.org).

The Letterboxing North America Web site includes online activities for kids and comprehensive easy-to-understand instructions for setting and hunting letterboxes throughout the United States and Canada. Letterboxing is nowhere near as popular as geocaching in terms of the number of boxes or the number of registered participants; however, letterboxing is a very similar activity with many of the same attractions. Obviously, letterboxing does not rely on the use of GPS units, but some people would argue that the lack of technology in letterboxing is a distinct advantage. Letterboxing is also a terrific option if you are teaching or leading geocaching activities and want an alternative or introductory activity.

TRAIL TALE

Kevin

The first time I went caching with my two sons was also the first time I ever found a travel bug. It was a key fob imprinted with a likeness of Kokopelli, a Native American deity. After returning home, we typed the travel bug's ID number in to the geocaching.com Web site and learned that the creators of the Kokopelli travel bug wanted it to travel around the world. My sons immediately bombarded me with questions about Kokopelli. We consulted an encyclopedia and learned a little about the deity. Then we began looking up geocache sites in New Zealand, where we were headed on a family vacation later that year. Without any original intent to do so, my sons had found a travel bug, learned about a Native American deity, and researched the places we were planning to visit on our trip to New Zealand—in other words, they had spent the afternoon engrossed in learning about things that I would have been hard pressed to convince them were important before we found that travel bug! We deposited Kokopelli in a cache site in Auckland, New Zealand. To my sons' great delight, the cache we found, called Hobson's Choice, was disguised as a cow pie! For months afterward, we logged on to check Kokopelli's progress; its last reported home was a cache in Tasmania.

Orienteering and Rogaining The sports of **orienteering** and **rogaining** also bear similarities to geocaching. Orienteering and rogaining both involve racing between hidden control points, or controls. Participants use clues about the general location of the controls before searching a specific area for the actual control point. The primary difference between orienteering and rogaining is the scale; orienteering is conducted over shorter distances and is completed within two hours at the most, whereas rogaining is an endurance event conducted over many hours. Rogaining is less similar to geocaching in that the controls are often less hidden—in fact, the controls are sometimes highly visible checkpoints—but the principle of searching with a map and coordinates clearly embraces a significant component of geocaching.

Orienteering, established in Sweden toward the end of the 19th century, involves racing between predetermined points on a course using a map and compass. Orienteering has many notable similarities to geocaching. Orienteers hunt for hidden controls that are difficult to find and that require participants to hunt around for them. Unlike a geocache, an orienteering control is simply an orange and white marker. The marker does have a unique "punch" attached to it that the orienteers use to prove that they found and visited that particular control. This is somewhat similar to the concept of logging a cache and marking the fact that a particular point was found and visited. Interestingly, the traditional orienteering control punch (a small plastic punch used to mark a unique pattern of holes in a piece of paper) is gradually being replaced by a high-tech punch that uses similar technology to the handheld GPS units used by geocachers.

✖ Orienteering, like geocaching, can be structured to include people of all abilities.

Orienteering and geocaching both involve participants using clues to lead them to the vicinity of their ultimate aim before pinpointing the exact location. A further similarity is the emergence of variations on the initial activity. Just as geocaching has diversified through the creation of many kinds of caches, orienteers have also introduced variations to orienteering. Because orienteering evolved from cross-country running, this activity was initially conducted on foot. However, many orienteering events now involve using mountain bikes, skis, and canoes or kayaks. More recently, orienteering events have also started including trail orienteering, which involves the use of hard-packed trails and is designed to allow people using wheelchairs or walkers to participate in the sport.

Appeal of Geocaching

The universal appeal of geocaching is remarkable. Although no statistics have been published on who typically goes geocaching, collectively the authors of this book have a very broad range of experience and can attest to the wide ranging appeal of this activity. Geocaching is hugely popular among families. Some people even plan their family vacations around collecting new caches. If a family shares a GPS unit, then geocaching can be a very affordable family activity. Geocaching can be great fun for kids and parents alike.

✖ Geocaching can make a fun and educational family outing.

Geocaching has also become increasingly popular among businessmen and businesswomen. In large metropolitan areas, geocaching is a popular lunchtime activity. It provides a wonderful way to take a break from work and get some exercise—while bagging another cache! Geocaching is popular among business travelers who can use it to fill evenings spent in hotels away from home. Many geocaches are placed in locations that appeal to the business traveler, such as around convention centers, major hotels, or large corporate headquarters. People from all walks of life are creatively combining geocaching with work through business travel, lunchtime breaks, or transit to and from work.

Geocaching provides educational benefits that make it a popular activity with school groups. It can be used to promote physical activity, to teach critical thinking and problem solving, or to deliver content from other areas of the curriculum. For the same reasons, geocaching is popular with after-school programs, church groups, parks and recreation programs, YMCAs, YWCAs, and other entities that provide care for kids. School groups can use this activity on campus to introduce children to coordinates, to teach latitude and longitude, to cover aspects of physical or social geography, and to help students build social skills by having them work together. Field trips are a great way for schools to use geocaching. Historic sites and monuments are a popular place for geocachers to hide a cache. By searching for these caches, children can discover the historical significance of a given area or monument. Visiting sites of historical interest can be far more memorable and engaging for some children if they are involved in discovering certain aspects of the site for themselves. In addition, geocaching is easily adaptable to a group activity in order to safely keep track of the children.

Recreation programs can use geocaching to promote physical activity or to provide an adventure experience for children, youth, or adults. By incorporating some of the different variations on a traditional geocache (as explained in later sections), recreation programs can provide challenging activities that are suitable for almost any community group. Geocaching could be used to focus on problem solving, mystery, or adventure. The activity can be tailored to an individual, group, or team challenge. In short, the many variations of geocaching provide an enormous degree of flexibility that enables recreation specialists to structure the activities to meet any client's needs.

Geocaching is also popular among college students and technology nerds who love to use gadgets. Although it is possible to keep the technology to a minimum (by using a basic GPS unit and writing out the coordinates of the caches you want to visit), the true technology lovers can really feed their passion. Many GPS units will now interface with a computer, and download-able graphing software packages are available to track the number and type of caches you have visited. This software can also compare your statistics to those of other geocachers through online forums. You can download geocaching applications to a smart phone and receive instant messages when new caches are added in your local area. Although technology is inevitably involved in geocaching, this activity seems to be equally popular among groups who are not known for living on the cutting edge of technology—many grandparents and retired people are passionate about caching.

For some people, the attraction of geocaching is the adventure; for others, it's about the challenge and competition of gathering as many caches as possible or gathering more caches than someone else. Many people find geocaching attractive because of the social benefits of going caching with other people. Other geocachers engage in the activity for the simple love of a good walk or the love of being active outdoors—regardless of whether they are in an urban or wilderness setting. Whatever their motivation, an ever increasing number of people are finding a reason to get involved in geocaching.

Types of Caches

Numerous types of geocaches exist. As geocachers get more creative, new kinds of caches begin to appear. A detailed discussion of the various kinds of caches is provided in chapter 4, but the main types of caches are traditional, multistage, mystery, event, benchmark, and grandfathered caches.

Traditional Cache

A **traditional cache** was the first kind of cache to emerge. This is the most common and the most easily recognized type of geocache. A traditional cache is some form of waterproof container that is used to store a logbook, a pen or pencil, and a few trinkets for people to exchange. The size and type of container used for these caches vary greatly, ranging from **microcaches** (such as a 35-millimeter film canister) to large caches (such as a five-gallon bucket or a sprinkler system control box). Geocachers are remarkably creative with the containers that they use. Many will modify a standard container to look like something that is common to the area where the cache is concealed. People who don't feel creative enough to disguise their own container can now buy geocache containers that are already disguised. When these containers are placed in a hole in the ground, they look like a piece of tree bark, a leaf, or maybe even a cow pie. A traditional cache, particularly one that is disguised creatively, is often the preferred type of cache for families and kids. If you are teaching an introduction to geocaching, then this is the first kind of cache that you should use. With beginners, you can start by placing a few of these caches for instructional use only. Hide the caches at the start of an instructional period, and have participants find them either in groups or as individuals. Remember the general principle that larger caches are easier to find. Have beginners start with large traditional caches before progressing to the microcaches, which are more challenging and difficult to find.

Multistage Cache

A **multistage cache** involves multiple cache sites. Participants collect clues from one cache site, and these clues lead them to another cache. Each cache provides a piece of information that ultimately leads to the final cache in the chain. This is an excellent form of caching for programs with an educational focus, because each cache can contain information that is critical to answering a question. This type of cache is ideal for small groups or teams and would therefore be ideal for Scouting groups, guide groups, church groups, or camps. You can use multistage caches that are published on the geocaching.com Web site if there are any in your area. You could also make your own multistage caches. This is a popular type of cache for families with older children; it's not so popular with younger children who can easily lose interest.

Mystery Cache

A **mystery cache** is similar to a multistage cache in that it may involve visiting multiple locations and it has a strong problem-solving component. The difference is that the problem solving—the mystery—becomes the central component of the cache. Each mystery is different, but the mysteries typically require the cacher to know something about a particular location, historical event, famous author, or some other topic (the possibilities are endless). A typical example would be that a story provides clues that make sense only when a person stands at the location divulged through the coordinates provided with the cache description.

In one specific example, the coordinates lead to one end of an island in the middle of a river; this spot is accessible only by a small watercraft such as a canoe. The cache description consists of a story that provides the cache coordinates, leading to a secret location described in relation to landmarks on the island. Geocachers must paddle to the location designated by the coordinates; then they must use the story to solve the mystery of the secret location. In one final mysterious twist, the cache is locked with a combination lock, and the code to the lock can be found on a paddler's life vest, or PFD (personal flotation device). All PFDs that are coast guard approved have a common identifying code. The last line of the cache's clue says, "Remember your PFD!" So the geocachers open the combination lock by entering that common code number.

Solving the mysteries or puzzles associated with a mystery cache may take time and some independent research. Therefore, this type of cache is ideal for educational settings. Solving the puzzle to find the next location could be assigned as a homework assignment. Both mystery and multistage caches are also ideal for after-school programs because they can be used to reinforce elements of the school curriculum in a fun and engaging physical activity.

Event Cache

The **event cache** makes a great field trip for any group or individual who is new to geocaching. An event cache is a gathering of geocachers who are excited about their hobby. At the event cache, participants share their enthusiasm and their experience in geocaching. Event caches are often attended by families, and they often take place at parks, playgrounds, or other kid-friendly locations. Many event caches involve potluck-style cookouts. These can be a great deal of fun. Some event caches are organized around the Cache In Trash Out (CITO) program that has long been promoted by geocachers. This program involves geocachers meeting to clean up a public area by picking up trash and helping with maintenance projects. CITO is a core value that the geocaching community embraces; all geocachers are encouraged (through the geocaching.com Web site) to make sure they pack out trash from the locations they visit while geocaching. An event cache organized around CITO is an ideal cache for any group with a commitment to public service, such as Scouting groups, church groups, Boys and Girls Clubs, or parks and recreation departments. Event caches can be of various sizes depending on their location and who's organizing them. Some are **mega-event caches** with more than 500 people attending. A mega-event may be organized on a regional or national level.

Benchmark Cache

Benchmark geocaching is ideal for groups that have an educational focus. A **benchmark** is a small metal disk (usually cemented into the ground) that is used as a permanent marker by the **National Geodetic Survey (NGS)** (figure 1.1). Benchmarks are points that can be pinpointed very

✖ **Figure 1.1** A benchmark cache in Cumberland Gap, Tennessee.

accurately, and they are used by map makers to survey an area. Benchmarks are useful in teaching map reading and cartography; they make a great geocache for people who are somewhat advanced in map reading and GPS navigation—and people who love the challenge of a cache that's difficult to find. A benchmark cache is definitely NOT recommended for young children. Children will not be able to exchange trinkets or even sign a logbook, and they are likely to get bored quickly when they realize that all they are hunting for is a small metal disk.

Grandfathered Caches

Geocaching has evolved since its inception. As the number and diversity of geocachers in the world have increased, so too have the variations on the types of geocaches that people place and like to visit. Certain kinds of geocaches were popular at various times but are no longer supported by geocaching.com. These include the locationless cache, the Webcam cache, and the virtual cache. Because they are no longer supported by the Web site, these types of caches have become known as **grandfathered caches**.

Perhaps the most popular of these grandfathered caches is the **locationless cache**, which has now become known as a waymark. A waymark is sometimes referred to as a reverse cache. **Waymarking** involves participants looking for items (waymarks) that fit a theme and then posting the coordinates of the items they have located. For example, you might set the challenge of finding statues containing or depicting animals. In response, people would take a digital image of any statue they found that met the challenge; they would then submit the picture along with the coordinates for the statue's location. Although waymarks, or locationless caches, are no longer hosted at geocaching.com, they are hosted on the Web at www.waymarking.com. Waymarking is a great family activity. Children will probably need help, and this is the kind of challenge that continues over an extended period of time. Waymarking could be a good challenge for a teacher to set as a summer assignment.

The **Webcam cache** was popular among technology-oriented geocachers, probably because it included multiple layers of technology. Although it is no longer supported by geocaching.com, Webcam geocaching remains an interesting activity for many people, and it might be a fun challenge for a family or for young adults. For a Webcam cache, the goal of the geocacher is to appear on one of the many Webcams that are live-streamed over the Internet. For a Webcam cache to work, the would-be geocacher first finds a Webcam that is viewable by the general public. The geocacher then lines up an accomplice to take a screenshot of that Webcam while the geocacher is standing in the camera's gaze. For example, popular tourist resorts often have a live Webcam that shows people how lovely it is on their beach or at their ski resort. So, when the geocachers are vacationing in that location, they would stand in front of the Webcam and call their accomplice.

They would ask the accomplice to log on, pull up that Web site, and take a screenshot of their smiling faces standing in front of the camera.

The images for some cameras are archived so that you can look back at what the camera was capturing at a particular point in time. If this is the case, then you don't need the accomplice to take your picture; you can simply record the exact time you stood before the camera and then later retrieve your image from the archives. Archiving Webcam shots is not as popular now as it was when live Webcams were new, but some cameras do still have archiving. Webcams are definitely not a cache for the technophobic!

The final grandfathered cache is the **virtual cache**, which is considered to be a variation of the locationless cache, or waymark. Like the location-less cache, the virtual cache is now hosted at waymarking.com. For the virtual cache, the waymark is not a specific item but rather the location itself. Because the actual location is the only reward for finding this cache, a virtual cache should not simply be an interesting or pretty location; rather, it should be something that is truly extraordinary or remarkable. For this reason, a virtual cache is often in a fairly remote location and can often be quite a challenge to find.

Benefits of Geocaching

Geocaching has very broad appeal and offers a wide variety of benefits. The benefits of involvement in geocaching will vary according to how a person chooses to engage in the activity, but the potential benefits are immense. Clearly, physical benefits are incurred when people become actively involved in the search, but people will also accrue important social benefits from engaging in the act of geocaching. The potential educational benefits are profound—a quick Internet search reveals powerful examples

Additional Equipment Needs

Always read the cache descriptions carefully for extra equipment that you might need to locate a cache. If the description indicates that a flashlight is needed, you might find the cache down in a cavern or inside a cave. If the description mentions a walking stick, you might discover that you'll need to reach farther than your arm can stretch to retrieve a cache. If the description says bring a calculator, there's a good chance that you will be solving clues involving multiple math equations. And if a boat is mentioned, you know you'll have to travel across water to find the cache.

of how geocaching can be used to teach history, geography, social studies, math, and science. Geocaching also teaches people to have respect for the environment through positive environmental stewardship.

Physical Benefits

One of the chief benefits of geocaching is that it involves being physically active. The level of physical activity will vary according to the person and the caches that are chosen. If you are organizing a geocaching experience or program, you can tailor the level of activity involved specifically to the individual or individuals who will be participating. Additionally, you can encourage participants to continue their involvement in geocaching independently as a way to integrate more physical activity into their life. By plotting a series of geocaches to be visited in sequence, you can create a course for groups or individuals to follow. Some participants might run the course trying to find the caches as quickly as possible; others might walk the course or run between some caches and walk between others. In short, geocaching can be used to carefully individualize the level of physical activity that people receive as a result of their participation.

Linking geocache locations as previously described creates something similar to an orienteering course; participants use the geocaches as a form of point-to-point racing in which the "race" is self-paced. In this scenario, varying the location and the type of cache would help maintain interest and allow the overall distance to be tailored specifically to meet individual needs. The fastest, fittest athletes would visit more cache sites over a far longer distance than the slowest nonathletes would. Simply resolving to hunt for a cache once or twice a week can help people increase their level of physical activity. People seeking to exercise through geocaching could vary their caching between parkland and urban settings or could use a combination of both. Varying the environment in which caches are being hunted is another way to build and maintain motivation.

Whatever the location, the distances involved, and the level of intensity of the participants, the element of adventure associated with looking for something adds a level of interest that makes geocaching more than simply running or walking. This element provides an additional benefit. In short, beyond the physiological benefits of the exercise, participants also receive the psychological benefits associated with the challenge and subsequent success of seeking and finding a cache.

Social Benefits

Many people feel a true sense of accomplishment in finding a cache, especially if it's well hidden. Children in particular can build self-esteem through the sense of accomplishment that comes with finding a geocache. This may be especially profound in children who are not well coordinated and perhaps not very successful in sports and more traditional physical activities. Geocaching gives people at all levels of physical ability an opportunity to be successful. It provides a form of physical activity that does not demand high levels of physical skill. In addition, geocaching offers the camaraderie that comes with belonging and being part of a group with common interests. People can take part in online communities of geocachers who discuss and exchange their geocaching stories, as well as event caches where geocachers gather in groups with other local cachers to socialize and talk caching.

The social benefits of geocaching are not limited to a sense of belonging or a sense of success and accomplishment at finding a cache. When used with a group of kids or adults as a group experience, caching can provide a powerful medium for developing group cohesion, building cooperation, and fostering communication. Recreation leaders, physical education teachers, and group leaders in a variety of settings frequently design activities to encourage group problem solving. This is a way to foster improved communication within a group of people who interact or work together. Geocaching provides an ideal forum for group challenges of this nature. A diverse set of skills is often required to find certain caches or perhaps to solve the puzzles within a mystery cache. As a result, a group often needs to call on the unique contributions and inherent strengths of all its members. The potential social skills learned in this situation make geocaching an effective activity for youth groups in various settings (e.g., church groups, Boys and Girls Clubs, after-school programs, and urban leadership settings).

✖ Geocaching is a great way to meet people and make new friends.

Educational Benefits

In many respects, the potential educational benefits of geocaching are limited only by one's imagination. Many popular geocaches (published on geocaching.com) are located at or near sites of historical or geographical significance. Many of these caches will contain information about the location. Some will focus on well-known information, while others will focus on more arcane trivia that will enrich the knowledge of those who find the cache. The process of setting a cache can also be very educational. If you are organizing a geocaching experience in an area of historical or geographical significance, you might set a series of caches that you don't publish—that is, you set them temporarily just for your group and do not list them on the Internet. You could also assign the group you are working with the task of hiding a temporary geocache for others in their party to find. In this case, you might add the stipulation that the cache must contain information about the significance of the location.

In setting or searching for a temporary cache, the geocachers must learn something about the area in which the cache is located. At its simplest, this will involve learning the basic geography of the area and perhaps discovering a road or trail that they had not explored before. In an urban environment, geocachers may discover a tree, a bench, or a memorial plaque they had never seen before. Geocachers may also discover a new hiding place within a familiar location. At its most complex, this will involve learning about the history or culture of a particular area. Whatever a cache leads to, the process of finding the cache will usually stir the geocacher's curiosity to the point of learning something. As geocachers learn more about the area in which they are caching, they will have a natural tendency to pay attention to the setting and their surroundings. Most people who go geocaching in the area where they live discover something new about a place they thought they knew, or they find out something new about their local environment. Geocaching in unfamiliar locations can be exciting from the standpoint of exploring somewhere new, but it will also often introduce you to aspects of a town or city that you might otherwise have missed.

Many instructional ideas are presented later in the book, but one of the most inventive ways to bring geocaching into the classroom is through the use of travel bugs. The basic concept is that a designated object, or **travel bug**, travels from one cache site to another by being picked up and dropped off by visiting geocachers. A travel bug is a **trackable item** that is easily identified by a dog tag–style label; the dog tag is stamped with the geocaching.com Web site and an identification number (figure 1.2). To create a travel bug, geocachers purchase a dog tag from the geocaching.com Web site and firmly attach it (by means of the accompanying chain) to an object of their choice. The travel bug is then registered on the geocaching.com Web site using the unique ID number listed on the dog tag. During the registration process, the travel bug's creator assigns a name, destination,

✂ **Figure 1.2** This travel bug, "Moe," had been traveling for 4 years when the picture was taken. Moe was last reported traveling through Europe.

and purpose to the travel bug. This information is stored on the Web site so people can look up the travel bug.

Travel bugs could be used to launch an instructional unit or theme within the school year by having the bug sent to visit sites around the country or the world. The sites that the travel bug is sent to visit might then be featured in some way through the curriculum as the school year progresses. For example, students studying the Civil War as part of a U.S. history class might send a travel bug out to relevant battlegrounds. The travel bug could include instructions asking the finder to take digital images of the battlegrounds and to post them to the Web site or e-mail them to the class. With careful planning, a teacher might have students help send out a travel bug at the beginning of a school year; this travel bug could visit key sites that will be studied during the year and then return to school by the end of the school year. Other examples of how travel bugs might be used to pique people's interest will be presented throughout the book (refer to chapter 4 for a detailed description of travel bugs).

The mere process of setting a new cache or registering a travel bug can itself be an educational experience, particularly for children and youth. The process involves rules and guidelines that must be adhered to before the cache or travel bug can become listed on the geocaching.com Web site. Aside from finding and reading all the guidelines posted at geocaching.com, a great deal of problem solving and a myriad of decisions are involved in setting a geocache. Decisions must be made about the type of cache, the precise location of the cache, and the type of container that is most appropriate to the cache site. With the traditional cache, decisions must also be made about the initial cache contents. Researching and designing a new cache could easily become a group project that will test the participants' social and group work skills.

Social studies is another popular content area for educators and activity leaders to focus on through geocaching. There is no need to travel for the activity—by placing a series of temporary caches in the ways described previously, you could have your geocachers discover a wealth of information about any given topic without leaving your regular meeting site. If you were running a kids camp on Martin Luther King Jr. Day, for example, a series of eight or nine temporary cache sites could be used to yield a wealth of information about Martin Luther King Jr. This information could in turn yield the answers to a series of questions about his life. In this example, the campers would all learn something about Martin Luther King Jr. while having fun geocaching and being engaged in an enjoyable physical activity.

Geocachers use a handheld GPS unit that relies on the use of coordinates for longitude and latitude, and the GPS unit is required to communicate with a series of orbiting satellites. These aspects of geocaching provide some obvious educational content in terms of geography, math, and science. Whether or not you are using geocaching in an educational setting, people's natural curiosity provides an opportunity for them to learn a great deal while being fully engaged in a fun and exciting activity. Simple **Cartesian coordinates** can provide a lead-in to explaining the coordinates used in geocaching. Even if you're working with children who cannot fully understand longitude and latitude, geocaching will enable them to see a practical application for the math of coordinates. In a similar fashion, you can introduce the many aspects of science that are embraced by the technology used in geocaching. These aspects take on added meaning when participants are engaged in the activity. Specific examples of integrating academic content into geocaching are addressed in part II of this book.

Environmental Stewardship

In addition to the educational benefits already addressed, one of the most powerful lessons that can be taught through geo-

TRAIL TALE

Peter

As I travel on vacation I am continually amazed at the number of historical facts I learn that I otherwise wouldn't know if it weren't for geocaching. For example, I have learned about Congressional Medal of Honor recipients at a dedicated glass wall in Indianapolis, Native American and U.S. soldier war heroes at Little Big Horn in Montana, a man who died at the Alamo from South Carolina, a story about why New Orleans is called the Crescent City, the first hydroelectric plant in Appleton, Wisconsin, and many other interesting facts. Thanks to geocaching, my knowledge and appreciation of history has been greatly enhanced.

caching is an increased awareness of, and respect for, the environment in which we live. By paying careful attention to minimizing the impact of geocaching on the environment and by cleaning up areas where people like to geocache, the geocaching community clearly shows that it values conservation and has a commitment to sustainability.

Geocaching has evolved around a healthy respect for our natural environment. This has included promoting cleanup efforts through programs such as Cache In Trash Out (CITO), as well as making people aware of the environmental impact of visiting a cache site. The geocaching.com Web site lays out guidelines and appropriate etiquette for setting a geocache. These guidelines involve paying close attention to the environment surrounding the cache site. The step-by-step guidelines for placing and maintaining a cache are very extensive and make caring for the environment around the cache site a clear priority.

In addition to the guidelines provided for identifying a cache location, the Web site also provides help on selecting a cache container as well as suggestions on content. You use an online form to submit all the details of your cache. Once you have submitted all the details of your proposed cache to the geocaching.com Web site, your submission goes through an approval process. Volunteer reviewers examine all proposed caches to ensure that they meet specified guidelines and appear to be a well-placed cache. Reviewers will look at the location of the cache to make sure it is not in a restricted or environmentally sensitive area. Reviewers err on the side of caution—if a cache appears to be placed in a fragile area or may be dangerous to visit (e.g., it appears to be too close to railway tracks), then it will not be approved and will not appear on geocaching.com. If a cache is refused publication, the submitter can revise it according to the reviewer's guidelines and then resubmit it. All geocachers are encouraged to report a cache that does not adhere to the published guidelines. For example, if the area around the cache site is being eroded by foot traffic to the site, the cache should be reported, and it will be removed from the geocaching.com Web site. Newly listed caches are often visited fairly soon after becoming listed on geocaching.com, and if the initial visitors report a violation of important cache-setting guidelines, the cache will not remain listed for very long. Generally, geocachers are very responsible and are good at policing a new cache.

Beyond geocachers valuing and respecting their environment, geocaching can be used as a very effective vehicle for teaching people about caring for their environment. Through cleanup initiatives such as CITO, geocachers model good environmental stewardship for their fellow citizens. The CITO program not only urges cachers to clean up as they cache and to pack their own trash, it also unites groups of geocachers in efforts to clean up areas of the countryside. This takes place in the form of an event cache or CITO cache that involves geocachers meeting at specified times and locations to clean up a particular area.

Conclusion

Given the enduring romanticism that surrounds activities such as treasure hunting, scavenger hunting, and hide-and-seek, it was perhaps inevitable with the advent of GPS technology that someone sooner or later would stumble across the idea of geocaching. Geocaching was clearly discovered sooner rather than later! Within days of selective availability being removed, geocaching had begun, and its growth since then has been nothing short of remarkable. Within 10 years of Dave Ulmer placing the first geocache (the Great American GPS Stash Hunt) on May 3, 2000, there were over a million active geocaches placed worldwide. With the increasing rate at which new geocaches are being registered, the second decade of geocaching promises even more remarkable growth.

Geocaching is an engaging activity through which you can touch on a broad range of academic content. Whether you are a teacher, a recreation specialist, or a group or activity leader, you can easily incorporate interesting educational components into any geocaching program or experience. When you consider that geocaching also provides physical activity experiences that are easily tailored to individual needs (in terms of time and intensity), it is easy to see that geocaching has a great deal to offer. Having developed a broad sense for the possible benefits of geocaching, you may already be formulating ideas of your own for how you might use geocaching. In the upcoming chapters, you will learn a great deal more about geocaching and will be introduced to a variety of learning and lesson ideas to stimulate your own creative potential.

HIGH-TECH
GEOCACHING

I n this world of ever-changing technology, people are always coming up with new ways to geocache. As soon as you get used to doing something one way, someone will introduce something new that leads to a better way of caching. High-tech geocaching is growing fast, and the possibilities are endless. This chapter covers some of the high-tech aspects of geocaching. It includes a discussion of GPS units and the basic features of a GPS receiver. The chapter also covers satellites and the triangulation needed to locate latitude and longitude coordinates. The use of computers, the Internet, and other technology is also discussed in this chapter.

GPS Units

Global Positioning System (GPS) units come with a variety of features. Some of the more desirable features include a cable so that you can interface the GPS with your computer, base maps for the areas where you will be using the unit, and sufficient memory to load maps and waypoints. A waypoint is a selected point of interest that can be downloaded and stored onto your GPS unit. The waypoint is basically the latitude and longitude (see the sidebar) of anywhere in the world, and the name of the waypoint is the object that can be found at that address (cache, airport, hotel, museum, and so on).

The computer interface will be invaluable as you get further into geocaching and start to hunt for more than one or two caches at a time. Base maps include general information about cities, roads, waterways, and some railways. Having sufficient GPS memory is important so that you can load

Latitude and Longitude

Latitude refers to the imaginary lines that run horizontally around the globe and are parallel to the equator. **Longitude** refers to the imaginary lines that run vertically around the globe, intersecting the North and South Poles. Altitude is how high above sea level you are at a given time. The first letter represents if it is North or South of the Equator and the second letter represents if it is East or West of the Prime Meridian. The numbers are represented in degrees, minutes and seconds. Here are some examples:

N 36° 34.720, W 83° 39.882

S 03° 48.061, W 38° 29.328

N 22° 35.224, E 114° 10.335

S 35° 11.107, E 149° 05.329

more detailed maps and waypoints. Some GPS units have extra memory cards that you can purchase. Most GPS units require either standard (AA or AAA) or lithium batteries. Be sure to always carry backup batteries as you head out to seek caches. You would hate to be out in the middle of the woods and have your GPS unit die on you. Many geocachers use rechargeable batteries in an effort to save batteries and keep from filling the landfills with toxic trash. If you have a color screen on your GPS, your battery life is much shorter than with a black screen. Many of the newer GPS units are waterproof or water resistant, so regardless of the weather, you can still get out and hunt. You can buy a GPS unit that suits the needs of geocaching for about $100.00. Many brands are available, and if you ask 10 different people what brand they like, you might get 6 different answers. The two main brands of GPS units are Garmin and Magellan, although there are others on the market that are just as good (figure 2.1).

Many of the new GPS units on the market are able to store up to 1,000 waypoints. Most are waterproof to some degree, and several have the Groundspeak Wherigo player application that will be discussed in chapter 4. Wherigo takes computer adventure games and brings them outdoors using GPS technology so you can have a location-based game. This is one way to enhance the geocaching experience. Wherigo cartridges are

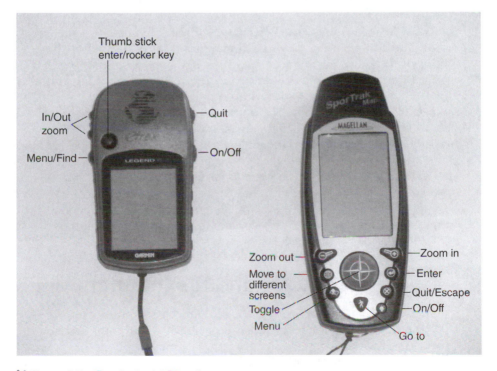

✕ **Figure 2.1** Two typical GPS units.

available at the www.wherigo.com Web site; these cartridges contain all the information you need to play out a Wherigo experience. A Wherigo experience can be anything from a city walk at historical sites to a tour of a university campus—the possibilities are endless. Several of the new high-end GPS models also come with touch-screen technology, which makes the units very easy to use.

A GPS unit can pinpoint your location anywhere in the world. The Global Positioning System is worldwide, but it is a utility that is owned by the United States. A total of 30 GPS satellites (as of December 2009) circle the earth in 6 orbit planes. These GPS satellites circle the earth in a similar manner to how the moon circles the earth. To obtain an accurate signal, your GPS unit needs to make contact with at least 3 of those satellites. Each satellite sends a signal that is picked up by the GPS unit; the signal gives a reading in latitude, longitude, and altitude of where that GPS unit is located on the earth. These satellites are positioned so that you can receive signals from at least 6 satellites at any given time, anywhere in the world (McNamara, 2004). To have triangulation, you need at least 3 satellite signals. The more satellite signals you have, the more accurate your readings will be. Most GPS units have 12 parallel channels to help acquire the satellite signals. The solar-powered GPS satellites have a life span of about 10 years; when one satellite is about to go out, a new satellite is sent up with new and updated hardware and software.

Most GPS units today can determine your approximate latitude, longitude, and altitude accurately to within 6 to 20 feet (1.8 to 6.1 m). Several things can throw off the accuracy of a GPS unit, including tree cover, power lines, tall buildings, cloud cover (to some degree), and the number of satellites that you have picked up (figure 2.2). Because the earth and the satellites are both moving, you may have a great signal one day, and then the next day, your signal may be obstructed by a tree, a mountain, or a building. If you are in the middle of a city and between power lines and buildings, your GPS may tell you to go one direction, and in the next two steps, it may tell you to go another direction. In this situation, you will want to get to as clear of a space as possible. Then you can try to get an accurate reading and can estimate where the cache you are looking for might be. After you have been geocaching for a while, you start to think, *If I were going to hide something, where would I place the container?*

Computers and the Internet

In addition to a GPS unit, geocachers also need a computer with access to the Internet. For geocaching, you will need to use the computer and the Internet to access www.geocaching.com. If your cell phone has Internet access, you can use your cell phone instead of a computer; however, it may not be as easy to read. In this book, we are assuming that a computer will be used for the majority of the time. Access to the Internet is becoming

✖ **Figure 2.2** Trees, tall buildings, and the number of satellites that you have picked up can all affect the accuracy of your GPS unit.

ever more prevalent. If you don't have Internet access at home, you can probably gain access through your local library. In addition, an increasing number of coffee shops are providing computers and access to the Internet.

As previously mentioned, although several Web sites promote geocaching and list geocache locations, the main Web site is www.geocaching.com. The geocaching.com Web site contains a wealth of information for beginners and experienced geocachers alike. For beginners, the Web site contains introductory information. For experienced cachers, the site hosts chat rooms and forums. And for everyone, the Web site lists a large number of caches from all over the world. We encourage you to visit the Web site, explore, and read. There are several ways to look up caches using the geocaching.com Web site. Once at the Web site, if you click on Hide & Seek a Cache, this will bring you to a page that enables you to look up caches in a variety of ways.

You can type in the physical address of a location, along with the parameters of how many miles away you would like to investigate. For example, entering "123 Main Street; Columbia, SC" and specifying within a 50-mile radius will produce a number of caches close to that location. You can also type in a city and state or a city and a country such as "Jevnaker, Norway" or "Pebworth, England." You can also discover caches by zip code and by state. For different countries, you can use the drop-down menu to select from about 260 countries. When you search by country, the results list all of the caches in that country starting with the cache that was placed most recently.

You can also search by state page. From a state page, you can see a list of events (recent past and future), the latest caches hidden, and the latest travel bugs and coins placed. You may also select to search by city (for cities with populations over 20,000).

If you know the latitude and longitude of the area, you can search for nearby caches this way as well. Several hotels and businesses have started putting their latitude and longitude on their home page. Other ways of searching include by keyword, area code, or waypoint. You may also search for caches that were found or hidden by certain geocachers.

Geocaching With Laptops

Laptop computers are getting smaller and much easier to use in a vehicle. They can be used with mobile access to the Internet or by saving a number of cache details and coordinates before disconnecting from the Internet. Laptops can also be used if you are out on the road getting several caches in an outing or on a geocaching vacation. Many people will load several waypoints into the **EasyGPS** software (free from geocaching.com) so that they are ready to spontaneously cache at anytime.

Geocaching With Google Earth

With Internet access and some creative thinking, it is possible (although not easy) for a person to go geocaching without a GPS unit. Cachers can do this by collecting the coordinates for a cache from the geocaching.com Web site and then typing the latitude and longitude into Google Earth. Using the zoom feature and the amazing image clarity available through Google

TRAIL TALE

Kevin

Geocaching is pretty high tech, but a friend of mine made it even more high tech when he went geocaching by helicopter! After I introduced him to geocaching, he noticed one cache that was refreshingly different—the owner of "Rock 'n' Roll" had grown tired of finding "junk trinkets," so he set a cache full of music CDs. The cache is a long way off the beaten path—it's an all-day hike there and back and is only visited once or twice a year. For a while my friend considered driving part way in his 4×4 and then taking his mountain bike up to the cache, but then the idea of flying in occurred to him. Borrowing a helicopter from his friend, he programmed the GPS and set off to trade a few CDs. He had to circle the area several times to carefully scout a safe landing spot, but before long he found a suitable spot not far from the cache and set down just a short hike away. He and his wife found the cache and came away with some new tunes after having taken all of about 30 minutes to get there from the local airport. Now that's some high-tech geocaching!

Earth, cachers can examine the environment around a cache site without leaving their computer. Armed with knowledge of the cache site and a mental image of the area around the cache site, geocachers can then visit the location in person and try to find the cache. This strategy would work best in larger cities where a greater number of photographs have been taken and stored on Google Earth. It is more difficult to use Google Earth once you get out into the suburbs and the country. Many cachers use a modified version of this technique by using the mapping option that is available through their free geocaching.com membership. By using the mapping option, the geocachers are able to get close to the cache before turning on their GPS unit. People who want to try geocaching before investing in a GPS unit—or people who are saving up for a GPS unit—can use this strategy.

TRAIL TALE

DuAnn

Remembering to write down or download the coordinates of a cache is essential, and not many geocachers will forget the coordinates of a cache. But the same doesn't automatically follow for other things! When hunting for a cache in a remote area where there's potential to get lost if you don't pay attention to where you're going, it's always handy to write down or plug in the coordinates of your car to the GPS unit. This, it seems, is not as easy to remember, as I know some geocachers who were so intent on finding a cache they forgot to pay attention to where they were going. Although they found the cache, they then promptly got lost and couldn't find their way back to the car for a couple of hours!

Finding Caches

You now have the basic knowledge to start your adventure. You have discovered that there are caches all around your home, school, and work. Let's get ready to go find some caches.

Downloading a Cache to Your GPS Unit

Now that you have your GPS unit and you've identified some potential caches on the Web site, you need to get them onto your GPS so you can go search for those caches. Each GPS unit is a little different regarding how to manually download caches, so you should be sure to read the directions for your GPS.

One way to put caches into a GPS is to do so manually—one by one and number by number. This is not the most efficient method, but you should learn how to do this on your GPS because there will be times when you need to manually put in the latitude and longitude. Every GPS is slightly different, so again, you should read your user's manual. For example, if you are doing a multistage cache (explained in chapter 4), you will need to key in the new coordinates for each of the next stages. As mentioned before, you really want to purchase a GPS that will interface with your computer because this makes downloading waypoints (cache name, latitude, and longitude) so much faster.

You can download multiple caches from geocaching.com in several ways. Use the computer cable that came with your GPS unit to hook your GPS unit into the computer. Read your user's manual to see how to do this, because there are many different ways to hook up the GPS to the computer. Depending on your GPS unit, you may need to complete several steps so that your computer will recognize your GPS unit. Chapter 4 gives you directions on how to log in to the geocaching.com Web site. You may want to go onto geocaching.com and follow along as you read the rest of this section.

As an example, let's say you have performed a search for geocaches by postal code. On the Web site, a page with a long list of caches (about 20) will appear. On the right-hand side of this page, a series of boxes will run down the page. If you click on a box, a green check will appear in that box; this means that you have selected that cache to download. Next, click on the icon to the right of the checked box; the icon looks like a GPS unit. Once the icon is clicked, that cache will be sent to your GPS unit.

Another way to download multiple caches is to use one of the free programs from **Groundspeak**, the official store of geocaching.com. This can be found by going to the Resources section of geocaching.com and then selecting Geocaching Software in the Tools and Downloads area of the page. Several programs are listed that you can choose from. Many cachers like to use the EasyGPS program. After downloading the program, go back to the page that has the caches listed for the area. Click on the boxes at the far right of the caches that you want to download to your GPS. Go to the bottom of the page and click on Download Waypoints; then click Open. The selected caches will then be sent to EasyGPS. Once you have the selected caches in the program, you can send them to your GPS unit, and you are ready to go search for the caches.

To keep from storing unwanted waypoints, you can use a little trick: In the comment or description area in the EasyGPS software, type in the city and state where the cache is located. Once you leave that city, you can easily go back to

![trail tale dashed line icon]

TRAIL TALE

Peter & Kevin

We both love paddling canoes and kayaks and recently heard about a creative way to combine our hobbies of paddling and geocaching. A whitewater kayaker making a solo descent of a long and technical river didn't have very much room to take supplies with him on his trip. Space was so limited that he befriended one of the guides at a local rafting company, who buried a small cache of supplies for him wherever they camped for the night. Each time he buried the supplies, he took a picture of his GPS unit over the cache site so that our intrepid paddler knew the coordinates of each precious cache site.

your GPS unit and delete those waypoints so they are not taking up space on your GPS unit.

After you have found a cache and either logged it in your computer or written it down, you should delete it from your GPS. Many GPS devices will only let you keep a limited number of geocaches, usually from 250 to 500 geocaches. Some of the new GPS units will allow you to download up to 1,000 waypoints. That may sound like a lot, but once you get into geocaching, you'll realize that it is nothing. For example, the city of Atlanta, Georgia, has over 4,000 caches in a 50-mile radius. Most GPS units will not support that many waypoints at one time.

Tracking Caches Along a Trip Route

If you are planning a road trip for business or pleasure, you can break the monotony of a long journey by bagging or logging a few caches along your route. If you think of this in advance, you can plan ahead and use the premium membership benefits of geocaching.com to map the caches along your route. If you are not a premium member on geocaching.com, you can still track the caches along your trip route, but it takes a little more effort. The first step is to go to the Web site and find a cache somewhere along the route, close to your starting point. For example, if you want to get caches along a highway, you would find a cache that is near the highway and pull that cache page up on the Web site. Next, pull up the map in the middle of the page and identify all the other caches near that highway. Continue to move the map and bring up the caches along the route. All the caches on the map frame will appear in a list to the right-hand side of the map. Click on those caches, download them, and keep going down the road. This takes time, energy, and patience to get all of the caches.

If you pay for the premium membership (see the sidebar), you can plug into geocaching.com and identify where you are traveling. If someone has added the route to the Web site, the site will quickly give you all of the caches along the way. This can cut down significantly on your screen time

Premium Member Benefits

Several benefits are provided to premium members on geocaching.com. The latitude and longitude of certain caches can only be viewed by premium members. As a premium member, you can bookmark your favorite caches that you have discovered. You can custom search based on cache size, location, and more. In addition, you can be notified by e-mail or cell phone when new caches in your area are added to geocaching.com. The cost for premium membership is a minimal amount (currently $30.00 a year).

and free up more time that you can spend bagging a few extra caches! If you have one of the latest smart phones, a growing number of inexpensive geocaching applications are available that will identify all the caches within a specified distance of your location. Although it's not so easy to plan ahead using this technique, you can search for caches on the fly—and if you ever find yourself with a little spare time, you can bag a new cache wherever you happen to be.

Using Maps to Find Caches

Many geocachers will use the Google Map from geocaching.com to locate a number of caches in an area. Once you are on a cache page, you can click on the map that appears about halfway down the page. This will open a larger map, and you can zoom in or out to see other caches in the area (figure 2.3). You can then print this page, and you will have the locations of several caches to take with you. The names of the caches will be listed on the right-hand side of the page.

You can get different views of the cache area. If you go to a cache page on geocaching.com and scroll down to the middle of the page, you will see a list of options under the heading For Online Maps. The options include Geocaching.com Google Map (this will list all nearby caches), MyTopo

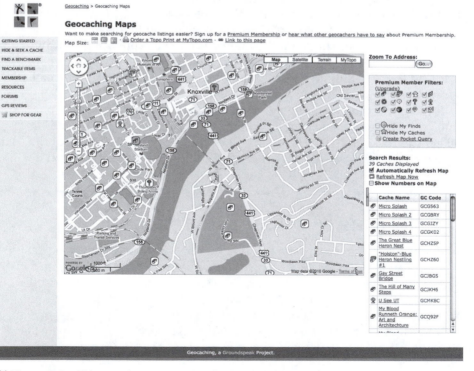

✖ Figure 2.3 This map from geocaching.com shows multiple caches in the Knoxville area.
Reprinted, by permission, from Geocaching.

Maps, Google Maps (sometimes has pictures), MapQuest, Bing Maps, Yahoo Maps, Rand McNally, Terraserver, and Tiger Census Maps. This list is continually changing and growing.

Another good source for online maps is ACME Mapper (http://mapper. acme.com). You can put in the latitude and longitude, and the online map will go directly to the cache site. This is similar to Google Earth in that it provides a three-dimensional image of the area.

Many GPS units come with a base map (showing major highways and lakes) and include the option of buying a CD with more detailed maps of specific areas that you can download. As you load maps onto your GPS, do not expect a very detailed map as you would get from a paper or Internet map. Some of the lower-end GPS units do not display maps well or at all. Many times cachers will also go by the "cheat" maps from geocaching.com (the ones listed previously such as MapQuest or Google Maps) or a car's GPS.

Combination GPS Units

A fairly new feature on each individual cache page is an option to send the waypoints to your phone. Not all phones support this technology. Consult with your local carrier. Some cachers are now using only their phone to go caching (mainly iPhone and Blackberry). The phone is their GPS unit and their Internet source, so they look up new caches as they travel. This is a handy feature if you travel and want to cache along the way.

Digital cameras come in handy when you are out caching. Some caches require you to take a picture of yourself and the object (or of the object and your GPS unit) and to post these pictures on the geocaching.com Web

✖ Geocachers can use a Blackberry to pull up the written information about a cache.

site. Also, you never know what you will come across while geocaching—a deer, a great view, or an unusual cache. Photography is another of the many hobbies that you can combine with geocaching. There are times when geocachers wish they had remembered their camera, but if you have a cell phone with a camera phone, then you are fine.

The use of an automobile GPS device has put even another spin on the caching adventure. When using this device, you have the turn-by-turn directions to get you to the cache site. As you are traveling, you should have already downloaded the caches located near the major highway that you are traveling on. This method enables you to easily see which exit you need to get off on instead of trying to use your handheld GPS unit (figure 2.4). Each automobile GPS has a little different protocol on how you will zoom in closer to the actual cache. Reading some of the forums on geocaching.com is a good way to learn about using this technology for geocaching.

You can download a cache to your personal digital assistant (PDA) in a portable document format (PDF) file; therefore, you will have all the information needed to cache paperless. As a result, you are not carrying lots of paper (i.e., your printed map and your pages of caches) as you are searching around for the cache. You just have your GPS and PDA. When using both a GPS and PDA, you should make sure that the caches that you downloaded to both units have the same name. This will enable you to easily pull up the PDF file on your PDA to match the cache that is on your GPS unit.

Some geocachers have downloaded GPS software to make their PDA work as their GPS unit. This way, all the information is in one location. Using a PDA as a GPS unit has several advantages. PDAs have an expand-

✖ **Figure 2.4**
Caches along a driven route. The four flags are the caches along I-75 at this particular exit.

able memory and can hold more information than a standard GPS unit. PDAs also have a larger color screen with higher resolution than a standard GPS unit. A couple disadvantages are that most PDAs are not waterproof and are not durable if dropped. Waterproof and shockproof cases can be purchased from various companies. In addition, most PDAs are powered by an internal battery that has to be charged, much like a cell phone. For a PDA to be used as a GPS device, special cards called GPS receive cards are required, and these cards use quite a bit of the battery life.

Conclusion

Geocaching will usually involve the use of technology. Most geocachers need to have a GPS unit, a computer, and access to the Internet. Information for the caches you want to find must be loaded onto the GPS unit. This can be done manually or by downloading the information from the geocaching.com Web site. Geocaching software can also be used to make the process easier and more efficient.

Technology in the geocaching world is growing fast and will continue to grow and expand. Some of the recent developments in technology include the ability to get a listing of nearby caches on your iPhone or Blackberry. This will take paperless caching to a different level, and the possibilities are endless.

chapter 3

LOW-TECH GEOCACHING

eocaching is technologically advanced when performed as originally intended—that is, with a GPS unit and regular access to the Internet. As explained previously, however, it is possible to geocache without the technology. If the participants you are working with are too young for high-tech geocaching and you need some lead-up activities—or if you don't have GPS units—don't let that hold you back. Several low-tech alternatives can provide wonderful lead-up and introductory activities when teaching or introducing geocaching. Low-tech alternatives, although they might not officially be geocaching, offer many of the same benefits and attractions. These activities can prepare people to engage in geocaching as soon as they are able. Some of these low-tech alternatives were introduced in chapter 1 in the historical context of being forerunners to geocaching. Some of those same activities will be expanded on here, and a few additional activities will be introduced. In this chapter, letterboxing is explained in more depth, and the concept of urban letterboxing is introduced. This chapter also covers the various forms of orienteering, including traditional, urban, and landmark orienteering.

Letterboxing

As introduced earlier, a curious—some might say bizarre—activity that is very similar to geocaching emerged from Victorian Britain. This activity is known as letterboxing. A cross between orienteering and treasure hunting, letterboxing emerged around 1854 as a little-known pastime of walkers and ramblers centered in Dartmoor National Park in South West England. For a long time, letterboxers apparently tried to keep their sport to themselves; very little seems to have been written about the activity. With the advent of digital communications, word is out and the activity seems to be catching hold.

Traditional Letterboxing

A traditional letterbox consists of a container similar to a geocache (figure 3.1); it typically contains a notebook and a unique rubber stamp. Letterboxers carry their own notebook, rubber stamp, and inking pad. When participants discover a letterbox, they put their own stamp in the letterbox's notebook and then use the stamp from the box to stamp their personal notebook. Calling letterboxing a sport is really a stretch under our usual notion of what a sport is. Letterboxing came into being spontaneously, and the only thing keeping it going is the people who participate. Clearly, letterboxing has the potential to yield many of the same benefits as geocaching, and for some people, it remains a novel and fun way to get some physical activity.

✖ **Figure 3.1** You don't need to be high-tech or gifted at hiding things to leave letterboxes for people to find. This message box is an example of a "low-tech" alternative to a high-tech geocache.

Traditionally, letterbox clues were placed in other letterboxes or passed between friends and acquaintances. Nowadays, like most things, they can be found on the Internet. A number of Web sites are dedicated to letterboxing in various parts of the world, including the historic home of letterboxing in Dartmoor, England. The following sample clues are for letterboxes in Dartmoor, England (Granstrom, 2006):

- ✖ Favorite Lunch Spots No. 22, Shapley Tor. Lone tree by road 312 degrees. Huge square boulder 346.5 degrees. Hut circle 277.5 degrees.

- ✖ Reynard's Happy Hour. Bellever 341 degrees. Hay Tor 51 degrees. Track disappears over hill 101 degrees. Under large rock half covered with heather.

- ✖ Dartmoor's Lost Unicorns No. 5–Hero, 5377, 8473, Have Feet Will Travel, FP 205 degrees. Cross 18.5 degrees. Large chimney on farm 241 degrees. Tip of dead tree 315.5 degrees. Tip of pointed rock 70 degrees and 9p away. Under rock on edge of clitter.

Reprinted from www.letterboxing.org/Smithsonian.html

The last of these clues is composed of the following information: The name of this course or clue is "Dartmoor's Lost Unicorns No. 5–Hero." The clue setter's nickname is "Have Feet Will Travel," the two numbers (5377 and 8473) are map references, and the rest of the clue refers to visible features within the area of the letterbox. The letters FP stand for flagpole; the rest are self-explanatory. According to Granstrom (2006), these sample clues are in the original letterboxing format. In the absence of a formal governing body and with the increasingly larger groups of participants, the clues have now evolved somewhat from the original format.

Although clearly different from the original format, the modern clues that we found online for North America maintain much of the original fun, and they certainly offer an intriguing challenge for any would-be letterboxer. The problem solving and the critical and creative thinking that go into setting and finding letterboxes could provide a wonderful challenge for people of various ages and in various settings—from kindergarten to the local church camp, from school settings to leisure, recreation, and other types of social groups. Here are three modern-day samples of letterbox clues that were adapted from clues listed on the letterboxing.org Web site.

✖ A good beginning letterbox, this one is easy to find. From the northeast corner of the senior center, walk toward the swings in the park. As you reach the horseshoe field, you will see two horseshoe posts and their backstops in front of you. The box is behind the left one under a rock. You will find four stamps and need only a pen and an ink pad. Be discreet.

✖ From the fountain by the church, walk forward toward the statue of the Virgin Mary. Now visit Father Brown. Walk toward the other fountain in the middle of the square. Next, turn around and walk up the stairs to the right toward Grand Avenue. Walk up six steps, and reach into the rear corner of the flower box under the evergreen bush to retrieve the box.

✖ A wayward, silly goose wandered up to this popular play area for dogs. Jasmine is a dog who was running by and stopped to sniff the goose. Of course, the goose didn't want Jasmine that close, and so the chase was on. They made their way up the dirt path toward the Open Space area. They made circles around the pull-up exercise bars, then went on through the opening in the fence. There were two trails, and the goose chose the one to the right, heading toward the closer hills. Jasmine noticed that she was almost in line with a very large power structure in the field. And when she wasn't looking, the goose found a rock grouping there on the left with the largest rock about 4 feet across and "rusty" on top. There were lots of loose rocks behind this large rock, spreading a couple feet more down the slight slope. The goose went to the corner away from the trail, that points closer to the lake than the other corner. There was a smaller rock (basketball size or so) that helped to make this corner a nice hiding spot, with smaller rocks piled on. (When going back to check on the goose, Sun Seeker counted 187 steps from the fence opening.) This rock is just right for sitting on, so please rehide the box well.

Second sample reprinted, by permission, from Sierra Sally. Third sample reprinted, by permission, from Cathy Wilcox.

This final clue, though a little long, offers an intriguing idea for teachers and recreation leaders who teach geocaching to kids—the idea of incorporating stories and story telling. The themes for stories could be seasonal or could address content from other subjects within a school curriculum.

The art of letterboxing could easily be modified further in a number of ways to suit a variety of settings. Laminated cards could be hidden before a class or training session for the participants to retrieve at the end. The cards could be concealed in obscure places, and clue sheets could be constructed to help students or participants find the cards one after another. Clues might be written in a form similar to the letterboxing examples previously discussed. This would provide an opportunity for students to practice and hone their compass skills. For easy courses, the cards could be made fairly visible. For difficult courses designed to test the abilities of skilled compass users, the cards may be fairly well hidden.

TRAIL TALE

Kevin

Orienteering is a great lead-in activity for geocaching or an alternative activity for geocachers. Orienteering involves hunting for hidden points called controls that are laid out to form a course, which orienteers follow using a map and compass. The low-tech alternative of the compass isn't quite as helpful as its high-tech counterpart, the GPS unit. While orienteering as a college student, I once got lost in a forest when it snowed heavily and made the map much harder to read. After being lost for an hour and a half, I finally gave up and backtracked to the start, cold and disoriented!

Urban Letterboxing

In certain urban settings, the placement of letterboxes or even a laminated card may not be practical. When this is the case, a modified version of letterboxing can be performed using a course made up of permanent features of the urban landscape. You provide seekers with enough information so they can figure out the approximate location of your clue site; the seekers must then use a compass and the urban landscape to determine the precise location. Once the clue site has been precisely located, the seekers could answer a simple question about that location instead of doing the usual stamping. An example of a clue for this kind of urban letterboxing might read as follows:

> Hydrant, G4, north corner of baseball field 120 degrees. Flagpole 304 degrees. Antenna 80 degrees. Face north and count how many treetops you can see over roof of bank.

The answer to this clue is the number of treetops that are visible when a person is standing in the precise location identified. If the participants are on familiar territory (e.g., students in a class), they could initially begin to locate this clue by moving to a place where they could see the north corner of the baseball field and a flagpole. Having no physical object to hide provides many advantages for people setting courses in urban locations—

My wife and boys went hiking and took along the GPS unit to find a cache. Much to our oldest son's delight, when they found the geocache they were looking for he discovered it contained a Pokémon card! Remarkably, given the number of cards he has, it was a card he didn't have in his collection. He was so thrilled that now whenever we go geocaching, he places duplicate cards from his collection in caches for other kids to find.

there is no need to find hiding places that won't be discovered accidentally, there is no container that has to be monitored or maintained, and for those operating on a tight budget, a whole course can be set without incurring any cost.

In many respects, this form of low-tech geocaching is similar to a virtual cache without the GPS coordinates. A course that includes eight or nine clues within a school campus could provide a challenging and instructive experience as part of a geocaching, orienteering, or outdoor education unit. From an experience like this, students would gain the benefits of physical activity, an increased knowledge of the environment around them, an opportunity to apply critical thinking and problem solving, and the chance to refine their compass skills.

A more challenging urban adaptation of letterboxing might require the participants to provide more detailed information about the specific point from which bearings originate. For example, if the clue leads participants to a spot in front of a statue, the assignment may be to research some aspect of the person depicted in the statue. For more mature and independent students, each clue could lead to research assignments designed to have students pursue independent research outside of class. This kind of course would also be great for field trips. If a school takes a field trip to a certain location every year, once the course is established, the preparation would be as simple as printing enough clue sheets to take along on the field trip.

Orienteering

A GPS unit is a remarkable piece of technology that replaces not only the compass but the map as well. However, as we all know, technology can fail. Therefore, people need to learn good map and compass skills even in the age of GPS technology. Learning these skills will also deepen a person's understanding of how the technology works. The modified letterboxing courses described in the previous section would provide a great introduction to geocaching with the added benefit of providing a framework within which to develop map and compass skills. In the previous examples, simple map-reading skills such as orienting the map, discerning topographical features, and interpreting the map's scale can all be developed in the hunt for the desired location. And once the participants are in the correct spot, they are then required to use the compass to take a number of simple bearings.

Orienteering is another activity identified in chapter 1 as a precursor to geocaching. Like geocaching, orienteering is an adventurous form of scavenger hunt. Competitors use clues along with a map and compass to search for predetermined points—called controls—that are laid out along a course. At each control site, organizers hang an orange and white control marker for competitors to find; each control marker is accompanied by a punch that competitors use to prove they visited that control. In its original form, orienteering is a cross-country running event, but it can easily be adapted to the urban setting for a fun, instructional activity that would be a wonderful lead-up activity to geocaching. The following sections provide a brief introduction to orienteering, followed by examples of how orienteering can be modified for urban environments.

Traditional Orienteering

Orienteering is a tremendous lead-in to geocaching for many reasons beyond the obvious similarity with geocaching and the fact that it provides a low-tech alternative. In many European countries, orienteering is very much a family affair; whole families often participate at the same event, and they sometimes run courses as a family. Orienteering is not as popular in the United States. Fewer clubs exist and far fewer events are staged each year in the United States than within a typical European country. Here are some of the most appealing features of orienteering:

✗ Orienteering is an inexpensive and safe means of pursuing an adventure-oriented physical activity.

✗ Orienteering is a non-elitist sport with a surprising number of active clubs offering events that welcome and help newcomers.

The International Orienteering Federation (IOF)

The IOF was founded in 1961 with 10 founding members. It now has 70 member federations all over the world—remarkable growth for an organization that is not yet 50 years old! The IOF Web site (www.orienteering.org) lists contact information for every member country, making it easy for you to find out about orienteering events wherever you live.

✖ As a club activity, orienteering provides the opportunity to meet people with similar interests and backgrounds.

✖ Orienteering represents a clean, back-to-nature experience in beautiful outdoor settings.

✖ Participation in orienteering is both a physical and mental challenge—orienteers like to call it cunning running.

✖ Orienteering can be pursued individually or in teams, competitively or noncompetitively.

Competition at events is usually keen but is always structured according to age, experience, and level of technical ability. People participating for fun can do so in the same area as people participating for the thrill of competition. Events are organized with a series of color-coded courses offered at different levels of difficulty from simple to complex; courses will be labeled as white, yellow, orange, red, green, blue, and brown.

Orienteering events have a single event clock, and staggered start times are organized around this clock for each participant. As participants arrive at the event, they register for a start time; these are offered every minute (or at busy events, it may be every 30 seconds) between the beginning and the end of the event. Events often begin at 9:00 or 9:30 a.m. and end around noon. This allows time to set up the courses before the event, and it leaves plenty of daylight afterward for people to finish the event and for the courses to be taken down. Having registered for a start time and a course at an appropriate level of difficulty, participants will receive a blank map and a set of control descriptions, which are essentially clue sheets describing the exact location of controls on their chosen course. When participants start their course, they have a blank map, their control descriptions, and a compass. Note that their map does not yet show the location of the controls that form the course they are going to follow (these locations are critical because the orienteers must use the combination of the map and the control descriptions in order to precisely locate the control markers).

The control description card shown in figure 3.2 is a typical example. At the top of the control descriptions are the title of the course, the color-coded level of difficulty, and the length of the course. The first of the three columns identifies the numbered order in which each control must be visited. The second column identifies the unique code that appears on the control marker (in this example, a two-digit number), which will instantly confirm to the orienteers that they have found the correct control. The final column contains a written description of the control markers' specific location. Control description cards that are more technical will also include a column containing the map symbol associated with the written description (e.g., next to "path junction," this column would contain two meandering lines in a T to symbolize the path junction).

✗ Figure 3.2 Orienteering control description card.

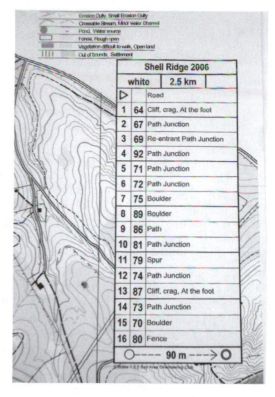

At the beginning of their race, participants race toward a set of master maps, which are usually laid out on the ground a short distance from the start. Being careful to visit the master map associated with their chosen course, the orienteers begin their race by copying down the location of the controls on their chosen course. Taking enough time to copy down the course accurately on their map is a very sensible investment of participants' race time! Courses are marked as a series of red numbered circles joined with a straight red line; the center of each circle represents the site of each control marker. The circle denotes the area in which the control is hidden, and the control descriptions provide a clue that leads to the precise location of the control. Starting with control number 1, the object of orienteering is to visit each control in order before proceeding to the finish line as quickly as possible. In the example from figure 3.2, the circle marking the location of control number 1 (not pictured) includes a crag jutting out from the side of a cliff. The control description informs the orienteer that the control is located at the base of the crag. Having successfully navigated to the crag marked by the red circle, participants would look at the base of the crag to find the control marker.

On easier courses (which are color coded as white or yellow), the control markers will likely not be truly hidden; once the participant has successfully navigated to the center of the marked circle, the control is usually found in plain sight. As the level of difficulty increases, the controls will be progressively more difficult to spot without using the control descriptions—they will certainly not be placed in plain sight. After discovering a control, the orienteers record the fact that they discovered that control by marking their control card with a punch (like the one shown in figure 3.3) that is attached to the control marker. Increasingly, the mechanical punches of old are now being replaced by electronic punches. However, in the context of using orienteering as a low-tech alternative or a lead-up activity for geocaching, mechanical punches are perfectly adequate. An electronic punch, or **e-punch**, is a device that senses the presence of a small electronic tag carried by each competitor; tags do not require power and are usually small plastic sticks that fasten conveniently to a participant's finger. When the orienteers locate a control, they pass their tag—often referred to as an e-stick—in front of the electronic punch. The e-punch uses **radio frequency identification (RFID)** technology to identify the precise time at which a particular orienteer visited that control. This allows fully automated, convenient scorekeeping to be used for an orienteering event.

The use of electronic punches eliminates the need for control cards (there is no need to punch your card because you prove that you visited the control electronically). But when mechanical punches are used, a simple grid of numbered boxes provides the participants with a means to prove they visited each control on their course. Printing a set of numbered boxes on

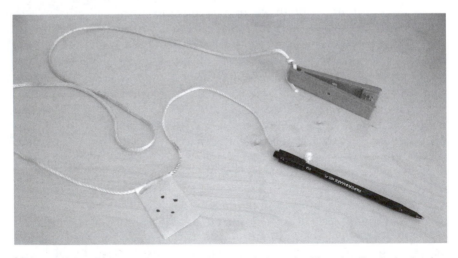

✘ **Figure 3.3** Participants can mark their control cards with a standard orienteering control punch (top) or with a homemade punch (bottom)—a pen, taped to a piece of string, which they use to copy a symbol from a piece of masking tape attached to the string.

the edge or the back of the map saves paper by incorporating the control card into the map itself. Again, in the context of a low-tech lead-up activity for geocaching, combining the map and the control card is a great idea because there will be one less thing for participants to lose.

Having punched their control card (or map) in the appropriate box, the participants proceed to the next control on their course to collect another punch. The simplicity of this concept makes orienteering a great introductory activity for the more complex world of geocaching. The prospect of buying orienteering equipment in the form of control markers, punches, and maps should not be a concern because you can easily and inexpensively make everything you need. Your first group of participants can even help make the requisite equipment. Figure 3.4 shows an empty plastic milk carton that has been converted into a control marker. Not only can control markers be made very inexpensively, but a pen on a piece of string can make a great substitute for an official control punch! A masking tape tab on the string with a pattern of dots drawn on it can be used to tell participants what to mark on their control card using the pen attached to the string.

Urban Orienteering

As an alternative to hanging controls in an urban area, an orienteering course can be planned using features of the urban environment. Urban orienteering is a terrific way to introduce map and compass skills because

✗ Figure 3.4 Two children mark a map with a homemade punch hanging from a milk-carton control.

many children are more familiar with the urban environment. Organizing an orienteering course for fun or instructional purposes does not have to involve going to a wilderness area or open land; controls can easily be hung around a school campus or an urban park.

Following the same principles as for a traditional orienteering event, participants choose a course that suits their level of experience and ability; they start the race with a blank map and a set of control descriptions. After copying down the controls (using the same course format of numbered circles) that lead around their course, participants navigate to each control site. When they arrive at a site, instead of punching a control, they write down the answer to a question. For example, a plaque on the wall of a building commemorating the day that the building opened would provide an ideal urban orienteering control. The control description might read as follows:

> Northeast corner of building, commemorative plaque reads ". . . opened on _ _ July, _ _ _ _ by . . . ."

By recording the day and year that the building was opened, the participants prove that they visited the appropriate control site. Other useful control sites are streetlights (the poles are often uniquely numbered), parking meters (which also have unique code numbers), and fire hydrants. Wherever the course is being set, there are likely to be interesting and unique elements of the environment that people frequently walk past without noticing. These elements often make great controls. This aspect of urban orienteering is exactly like geocaching—by completing the course, participants can learn new information about an area that they were already familiar with.

TRAIL TALE

Peter

Occasionally a GPS unit loses its magnetic compass bearings because an unusual magnetic field (such as one created by a lot of power cables) interferes with its functioning. When that happens, there is a button on the GPS unit that helps you recalibrate your compass. You go to that page on your GPS, click on "Start," turn around slowly two times, either clockwise or counterclockwise, and bingo—your compass is calibrated correctly again. I have often used this example in my own life to reorient myself. When I get too busy, confused, or pressured, I stop, take a deep breath, turn around two times, and move on with my life with a clearer vision of what to do next!

Landmark Orienteering

Many people have come up with their own version of landmark orienteering. Some might even view urban orienteering as a form of landmark orienteering. Regardless of how one chooses to label the activities, landmark orienteering is a wonderful variation on orienteering that can be used as part of an orienteering unit, as a fun challenge or fitness activity, or as a lead-up activity within a geocaching unit. Clearly, any form of landmark orienteering is going to involve finding landmarks; however, given that landmarks are easily recognizable and prominent features within a particular landscape, an effective method is to use photographs of each landmark in the clue. A good landmark control, like a well-placed geocache or letterbox, will engage the participant in a high degree of problem solving. Participants should be able to study the photograph—examining the background, middle ground, and foreground of the photograph—to find clues about the location from which the photograph was taken.

For the photograph in figure 3.5, participants who are familiar with the location of the orienteering course would instantly recognize the landmark in the background. Through careful observation and simple problem solving, participants would be able to deduce precisely where that particular view was taken from. In this example, participants would need to identify the two communications towers, the hill in the middle ground, the partially visible building and trees in the foreground, and, of course, the streetlight. Having discerned the features that make up the photograph, participants then have to think critically about where one would have to stand to see

✖ Figure 3.5 A sample landmark orienteering control. Participants use the clues in the photo to determine where it was taken. As proof that they located the correct light pole, participants will complete this clue: "The code on this light pole reads 'CP _ _ / PR _ _.'"

the mountain and the two communications towers in that particular configuration. The partially visible buildings and the road in the foreground provide additional clues. Once participants have figured out where that particular light pole is, they will record the unique code on the pole as evidence that they found the right one.

Learning careful observation and developing critical thinking skills are two of the primary benefits to be derived from this form of landmark orienteering; both these skills are important in orienteering and geocaching. Having participants make their own landmark orienteering courses can help them develop their observation and critical thinking skills even further. Although this will require your students to use cameras, the advent of digital technology has rendered the digital camera a fairly common and comparatively low-tech device. By varying the complexity of the photographs and the dispersal of the controls within the area you are using, you and your participants can make courses that involve a broad spectrum of ability levels.

Activities of this nature can be made developmentally appropriate for all ages and all stages of development. If you are working with young children, you could set up a "string course" with one very long piece of string attached to a series of controls. Lay out the string to lead participants through a confined and controlled area. Children can then safely and successfully follow the string to find the controls that are threaded on the string. These courses could be tied directly to concepts and content being addressed within the academic curriculum (based on the age of the participants you are working with). This type of string course would be suitable for preschool, day care, and kindergarten settings. It could easily be part of a school, after-school, or school holiday program.

Alternative Orienteering

All the low-tech activities proposed in this chapter so far have involved people seeking controls, letterboxes, or cache sites in a predetermined, numbered sequence. The concept of racing from point to point in this way is a fundamental tenet of a traditional orienteering course; however, other forms of orienteering have been devised that could also offer exciting lead-up activities for geocaching instruction. Some orienteering events are referred to as points events or score events. Such events sometimes have the same staggered start times where participants leave at set intervals, but occasionally they will have a mass start with a large group of participants starting at once.

In score or points events, all participants begin with the same set of control descriptions, and the total number of controls is far greater than in a traditional orienteering event. These events generally begin and end in the same location and last for a predetermined period of time, making them ideal for use in an instructional setting. The control descriptions contain point totals next to each control (figure 3.6). Large differences will exist

Cal Poly Urban Score Course

1 Fire Hydrant Number " _ _ "   20 points

2 Plaque on wall gives title of mural " _ " 1973.   20 points

3 Memorial stone in front of PAC reads " _ _ _ _ _ _ _ _ _ _ _ _ _ _ _ _ In memory of ..."   40 points

4 Assistive device for wheelchair access, model name is " _ _ _ _ _ _ _ _ _ _ _ _ "   40 points

5 Plaque on wall reads "The American Institute Of Architects _ _ _ _ _ _ _ _ _ _ _ _ _ _ _ _   40 points
   _ _ _ _ _ _ _ _ _ _ _ _ _ _ _ _ _ _ "

6 Memorial reads " _ _ _ _ _ _ _ _ _ _ _ _ _ _ _ _ " dedicated June 1977   40 points

7 Wheelchair sign at wall's end reads " _ _ _ _ _ _ _ _ _ "   40 points

8 Commemorative plaque reads " _ _ _ _ _ _ _ _ _ _ _ _ _ _ _ _ " In Memory of Dr. Robert   40 points
   E. Meyers Jr.

9 How many circular holes are there in the mirrored pyramid? " _ "   40 points

10 Street lamp pole number " _ _ "   40 points

11 Large dark green electrical box, code on plate at front South East side reads "SO _ _ - _ _ - A"   60 points

12 Memorial stone at base of tree reads "Cal Poly Commemorative Tree This Bronze Loquat In   60 points
   Loving Memory of _ _ _ _ _ _ _ _ _ _ _ _ _ _ "

13 Concrete Bench, inscription on dedication plate reads "In Appreciation to _ _ _ _ _ _ _ _ " 60 points

14 Fire Hydrant Number " _ _ "   60 points

15 Number set in sidewalk " _ _ "   60 points

16 Fire Hydrant Number " _ _ "   60 points

17 Memorial stone at base of tree reads "Cal Poly Memorial Tree In Loving Memory of   60 points
   _ _ _ _ _ _ _ _ & _ _ _ _ _ _ _ _ _ _ _ _ _ " "It'll Be OK "

18 Two green electrical boxes, words written in cement behind them " _ _ _ _ _ " & " _ _ _ _ _ _ "   80 points

19 Street lamp pole number " _ _ _ "   80 points

20 Fire Hydrant Number " _ _ "   80 points

21 Concrete bench dedicated to " _ _ _ _ _ _ _ · _ _ _ _ _ , Biological Sciences Professor"   80 points

Urban Score Course Master Map

✖ **Figure 3.6**   The map and some of the control descriptions for an urban orienteering score or points course.

between the lowest and highest point totals for controls; the point totals are in proportion to the distance the controls are placed from the start. The controls placed farthest from the start carry the largest point totals, and those closest to the start carry the lowest point totals. Therefore, participants must gauge how far they can go in the allotted length of time. Significant time penalties are incurred by participants who finish after the allotted time has expired, so runners who overestimate their ability risk losing all the points they gained from visiting the long-distance, high-point controls.

Score events can be set up using traditional orienteering control markers or using any of the various modified versions of a control presented in this chapter. For instructional settings, the controls described earlier for urban orienteering are perhaps the easiest and most practical. Although the initial task of identifying and mapping up to 40 control sites seems rather daunting, this task actually takes only a couple of hours. And the next time you use the course, the only required preparation is to run copies of the map and control descriptions, making the initial investment of time more worthwhile. This is in sharp contrast to a more traditional orienteering event, which can involve a great deal of setup and takedown time associated with hanging and retrieving the control markers.

The principles behind an orienteering score event could be mimicked in a geocaching event. To do this, you could provide students with lists of coordinates and corresponding clues and then allow a set amount of time for participants to gather as many caches as possible. Assigning point values to each cache would introduce a fun and motivating twist for geocachers.

Conclusion

Although there is no direct link with letterboxing in the historical development of geocaching, letterboxing is clearly based on the same principles as geocaching and bears a striking similarity. Letterboxing, either in its original form and settings or in its more modern form and urban settings, is a wonderful low-tech alternative to geocaching. Letterboxing could also be a great way to introduce geocaching to the people you are working with. Orienteering offers much the same appeal as letterboxing in terms of a way to lead into the more technologically intense world of geocaching. Laying geocaches in a course format similar to orienteering is also an intriguing idea. Running this type of course would give beginners the opportunity to learn and practice geocaching skills. For more experienced geocachers, setting this type of course is a great way to advance their skills.

All the lead-up activities presented here could be modified and adapted in the same ways that geocaching can be modified. Activities could be restricted to trails or areas that are wheelchair accessible, or they could be adapted for use in conjunction with bicycles, in-line skates, skateboards, or even skis. The low-tech alternatives to geocaching have varying degrees of similarity to geocaching, but each bears some similarity and offers many of the same benefits—and they all offer experiences that will whet peoples' appetites for this type of activity. Even as the rapid development of GPS technology makes high-tech geocaching more feasible for everybody (regardless of budget), the low-tech alternatives will provide challenging and fun activities that enable geocaching fans to hone their skills, get in shape, and enjoy a few quirky alternative activities.

BASICS OF
GEOCACHING

Now you are ready to learn more about the various types of caches. When you set out on an adventure of geocaching, you never know what you will discover. You may discover a new area or a type of container that you have never seen before. This chapter covers some of the common types of caches, gives you helpful hints to get you started, and describes how to log your find into the geocaching.com Web site.

What Is a Cache?

As discussed in chapter 1, a cache is something that is hidden for geocachers to find or discover. Since the inception of geocaching in 2000, the number of different types of caches has grown, and it will continue to grow as people become more caching savvy. As you read this, several other types of caches and containers will have likely been added to the geocaching world since the publication of this book. Just when you think you have seen it all, you will discover another type of container. Although there are different types of caches, most caches will contain certain items, such as a logbook and a sheet explaining geocaching. The bigger caches contain items for people visiting the cache to trade.

Caches that have a container to find will always include a log for you to sign. The size of the log may range from a small piece of paper rolled up to fit into a microcache to a small spiral notebook. When you find the cache, you sign and date the log using your geocaching name (more details will be discussed later in this chapter). You should always bring along your own pen and pencil when geocaching. If the cache is small, a writing utensil may not be provided in the cache. Other times the writing utensil provided may not be working properly. Before you head out the door, you should always check that your pens and pencils are in working order. You would hate to get to the cache site and not have anything to write with. After signing the log, you would then trade items if the cache includes trinkets to trade.

Most caches include a short note that welcomes the person to the cache. Many people who set caches will use the note provided on the geocaching.com Web site (or use a note similar to this one). This note is included on the Hide & Seek a Cache page of the Web site and is currently available in about 35 different languages. The note provides an explanation of geocaching that is mainly targeted to muggles. It describes what they just found and provides directions on what to do and what not to do with the container and contents. The note basically says that the person has found the cache either intentionally or not. It asks the finder not to remove or vandalize the container and to place it back where it was found. The note also lists the geocaching.com Web site.

Various items can be traded in geocaching (figure 4.1). Many people will bring a bag or a backpack with them as they go caching. In the bag, people

✖ Figure 4.1 You never know what you might find in a cache! Usually there's a log for you to sign, but otherwise, anything goes. This cache contains a lizard, a girl scout patch, an eraser, a compass, and a few other things.

typically carry items such as children's toys from kids' meals, rubber frogs, patches, CDs, matchbox cars, army men, small bouncing balls, or anything else that will fit into the container. Some caches are theme specific, and you should try to leave an item that fits the theme (e.g., maps, books, or CDs). Some cachers have their own signature items that they always leave, such as painted stones, small army men, patches, rubber frogs, or handmade items. You do not have to leave anything in the cache; you can just sign the log. However, if you take an item out of the cache container, then you should leave an item.

Special items such as travel bugs and geocoins may also be found in a cache. These items can be purchased from Groundspeak and other sources.

Travel bugs are items that are meant to travel from one cache to another as they are found by geocachers. A travel bug is trackable because of the unique tracking number that is stamped on the attached dog tag. Typically, the owner of the travel bug will give it a task or goal such as to travel to a certain place or certain places. The goal is identified on the geocaching.com Web site. Each travel bug has a page on the Web site where you can post information and pictures about the bug. In a cache, you may sometimes find the travel bug in a plastic bag, and it may or may not have an owner-made card attached to it with a statement about its goal. One cute travel bug is a little locomotive train that wanted to travel the world and see as many railroad-related sites as possible. This little train started off in South Dakota and at the time this was written had traveled a total of 17,167.9 miles. In addition to the United States, the train has traveled in the Netherlands, Germany, and Bulgaria—it has been across the Atlantic Ocean four times. The train was last in Michigan and has probably moved on to other adventures. Another travel bug is named Bear in the Big Blue House. The goal for this travel bug is to explore all around the world; the bear started off in Tennessee and at the time this was written was moving in the hands of someone in South Carolina. If you find a travel bug, remember that the idea is to keep it moving from cache to cache. Geocaching etiquette calls for you to take care of travel bugs when you have them and to help move them along on their journey.

Geocoins are logged the same way as travel bugs, using their unique trackable number (figure 4.2). These can be purchased from many sources (including groundspeak.com, amazon.com, and other sources listed on the geocaching.com Web site). The coins may have various impressions on one side, and they usually have the geocaching.com logo (yellow, green, blue, and orange) on the other side.

Part of the etiquette of taking travel bugs and coins is to move them to another cache soon after you have picked them up. If you can help the

✘ Figure 4.2 Geocoins are also known as *travel coins*.

travel bug along in its quest, then by all means help it along; however, if taking the travel bug will hinder the bug's intended journey, then you should not pick it up. For example, if you are caching in Virginia and you plan on heading to New Mexico, you should not pick up a travel bug if the bug's goal is to reach a place in Florida. Leave that bug for someone who can help.

Caching Etiquette: Top Eight Tips

As with any sport or activity, geocaching involves some rules of etiquette that all participants should learn and follow. Keeping these things in mind will help make geocaching fun for both you and others. Many of the following tips will start to become common sense once you really get into geocaching.

1. Be Stealthy

As you are hunting for the cache, you do not want to give away the cache location to others around you. As mentioned in chapter 1, muggles (those who do not know about geocaching) are more likely to take a cache if they find one. To a muggle, the cache is just a container full of goodies. Geocaching requires stealthlike movements. Think of this as a spy mission—you want to get in, sign the log, get the goods, and get out without giving away the location. However, you do want to be sensitive and make sure you do not look like a spy or look as if you are up to no good. You can pull out a trash bag and start picking up nearby trash. If you think you can grab the cache, you might act as if you are on your cell phone and try to be as inconspicuous as possible. Be aware of your surroundings and any other people around. If many people are around the cache site, you may have to leave the area and come back when it is not quite so busy.

TRAIL TALE

Katherine

Some cachers will try almost anything to find a cache! Once I was on an Alaskan cruise and, like any good cacher, printed off several that I might come upon during our 21-day adventure. In Skagway, Alaska, I went after a virtual cache at the Skagway cliffs. Fortunately, our ship was docked right next to the cliffs. However, there is a lot to look at to find this cache, because it involves searching through many ship names that have been painted on the cliff face. As I was looking, I went as far as the security guard would let me go. I tried to explain to him what I was doing, but he did not go for it. So I boarded the ship, took my binoculars, and went outside on different decks. From the top deck, I scanned the whole cliff face but couldn't find the information I needed. Then I went down a few decks and was almost eye level with the cache. After about 30 minutes I finally found the answer to the question and was able to log the find.

2. Determine Whether People Are Muggles or Cachers

As you are hunting for a cache, you will sometimes encounter another person who is moving in a way similar to yourself. Look for the signs of a GPS or phone being held down while the person is walking around. Do not be afraid to say, "Geocaching?" Many times the person will say yes, and then you can look for the cache together. If the person says no, then you might explain what geocaching is, and by the end of the conversation, you may turn this person into a fellow geocacher.

3. Stand Aside if You Find the Cache First

If you are caching with someone else or you happen to encounter another cacher, one of you will find the cache before the other person. In this case, the person who spots the cache first should move away and go stand away from the cache. This will give the other person a chance to find the cache as well. Typically, this is the procedure used when people geocache in groups; however, a group may sometimes specify that the person who finds the cache should let everyone know.

4. Leave the Cache Where You Found It

When you find the cache, sign the logbook and return the cache to its original location. Place the cache back just as you found it. However, you may adjust the cache's location if it appears to be out of place when you find it. For example, if you find the cache at the base of a tree and out in the open, you may discover on further investigation that the cache should be in the small hole right above the ground. Remember, you must not take the cache container.

5. Make an Equal Trade

If you are taking an item from the container, you want to leave an item that constitutes an equal trade. This means the value of the item you leave should equal the value of the item taken. For example, do not leave a little green army man and take a book. You might have to put in several things to equal the value of an item you would like to take.

6. Do Not Put Improper Items in the Cache

Some things should not be put in caches, including food and dangerous objects such as knives, guns, bullets, and so on. Remember that kids may be participating in geocaching with their families, so you want to make the contents of the container safe. Food may attract wild animals that will destroy the cache container. Use common sense when leaving things in a cache. If you find a cache that has an inappropriate item in it, you should take the item out.

7. Get the Property Owner's Permission

When placing a cache, you should make sure you get permission to place the cache from the property owner. This is especially true when using an old surplus ammo box. Many caches have been blown up by the police because they thought the ammo box was a bomb. If you are placing a cache at a wedding chapel, for example, you should discuss it with the owner of the chapel, explain geocaching to the owner, and get permission to place the cache. Many property owners enjoy talking to people who come geocaching on their property.

8. Always Put Safety First

Anytime you do not feel safe while caching, you should not proceed. On rare occasions, a cache might be located in an area that you do not feel safe traveling into. For example, in one area, a group of geocachers would have had to walk through a dark alley in order to get to the cache site. The group did not know a good way around, so they decided not to get that cache.

Types of Caches

Many types of caches exist, including traditional, multistage, mystery or puzzle, letterbox hybrid, Wherigo, earthcache, and benchmark. This list will continue to grow because people are always coming up with new types of caches.

Traditional Cache

The traditional cache was the first type of cache. This is the most common and the most easily recognized kind of cache, and it has already been discussed in various forms in this book. A traditional cache is composed of some form of waterproof container. The coordinates on the cache page of the geocaching.com Web site are the exact location of the cache. The size and type of container can vary greatly, but the caches are usually classified as micro, small, regular, large, and unusual or creative.

TRAIL TALE

Peter

A retired friend in South Carolina has dedicated countless hours to a local project converting a stretch of railroad into a hiking trail called the Palmetto Trail. The community has come together over the effort, working with the railroad company to develop the trail for public recreation; it's a real success story and a great place to go geocaching. A local scout troop has been helping with the project and has placed geocaches along the trail so that hikers, mountain bikers, school groups, church groups, families, or whoever can enjoy hiking the old railroad trail and have the added fun of finding geocaches along the way.

A microcache is typically a 35-millimeter film canister, an Altoid can, buffalo tube (long cache capsule), pill bottle, or a waterproof match container. Another microcache that can be purchased is called a Mr. Magneto, which is magnetized and measures .5 by .4 by .4 inches. Many caches are magnetized by gluing a magnetic strip to the container. This allows the container to be placed on metal objects such as under a park bench, under the skirt of a light pole, and on signs. Figure 4.3 shows a homemade magnetic bottle. Typically, microcaches only contain a small logbook.

A small cache is about the size of a Tupperware-style sandwich container (about a one-quart size) and generally holds a logbook and small trade items.

A regular cache is the size of a Tupperware-style or ammunition canister (ammo can) and usually holds a logbook and larger trade items. The ammo cans are sturdy and waterproof. They come in two basic sizes and can be bought at army surplus stores as well as flea markets.

A large cache is about the size of a five-gallon bucket or a large tackle box, although some may be larger. These large caches are not common, but there are a few of them out there.

The unusual and creative caches can be a variety of things, such as hollowed-out bolts, fake dog poop, fake water lines, fake signs in parking lots, fake bolts, hollowed-out logs, fake sprinkler heads, fake post caps, fake metal wall plates, or fake pine cones. Geocachers are getting more and more creative in how they hide caches. Just when you think you have seen them all, something new comes along that throws you into a spin (figure 4.4).

✖ Figure 4.3 This homemade magnetic bottle was found on the upper inside of a free newspaper stand.

✕ Figure 4.4 Caches can be disguised as just about anything. Here, a cache is disguised as a PVC box on top of a piece of electrical conduit.

Multistage Cache

Multistage caches are just what the name implies—you have to go to multiple places to discover the location of the final cache. Typically, the first coordinate leads you to the first container, and this container provides another set of coordinates that leads you to another cache container, and so on, until you find the final cache. The final cache contains the goodies and the log.

In another version of multistage caches, you have to visit various places in a specific order and answer questions on the cache page on geocaching. com by filling in the blanks based on clues provided at each site. Usually, you do this by finding numbers in the surrounding environment and placing the numbers in the appropriate spaces to solve for the coordinates of the next site (see table 4.1). The final set of coordinates leads you to the cache.

Mystery or Puzzle Cache

For a mystery or puzzle cache, participants must first solve a complicated puzzle or problem (e.g., a math problem) in order to determine the coordinates of the cache location. Because geocaching is growing so quickly, this category is also used for unique and new challenges. The information needed must be available to everyone; however, solving the puzzle or problem to discover that information will take some investigation. For this type of cache, the coordinates listed on the geocaching.com Web site are not the true coordinates. Fake points are given because a latitude and longitude are required in order to list a cache on the Web site (on the cache

Table 4.1

SAMPLE MULTICACHE CLUES

	Coordinates	Clues
Start	N 35° 59.782/W 82° 01.555	Solve for letters A, B, C, D, E, and F to determine the next stop coordinates. A through F are different for each stop.
Stop #1	N 35° 59.**A B C** /W 82° 01.**D E F**	F = Number of days payment required plus 1 B to D = Hours in effect D + 2 = A A – F = C = E
Stop #2	N 35° 59.**A B C** /W 82° 01.**D E F**	Year this "clock" was restored: EBAD (E = first digit, B = second digit, and so on) C = Number of wings F = West minus 1
Final cache	N 35° 59.**A B C** /W 82° 01.**D E F**	X = Number of columns X ÷ 2 = F 3F = A A – 1 = D B = Number of flagpoles B – 1 = E C = Number of stars

page, it is clearly stated that the cache is not at the coordinates listed). However, the fake coordinates should be within 2 to 3 miles of the true location of the cache.

For example, a very simple puzzle may involve a series of nautical flags listed in a row. These flags would be presented on the cache page of the Web site. You might also be given the following information: N 38° 01.ABC, W 82° 04.DEF. Each nautical flag has a letter equivalent in the English alphabet. You have to perform research to identify what letter each flag represents; then you identify the corresponding number of that letter in the alphabet to get your latitude and longitude. If you find out that the first flag represents the letter T and the second flag represents the letter B, you would then determine that T is the 20th letter in the alphabet and that B is the 2nd letter in the alphabet. Therefore, 20 would go into the slot of AB, and 2 would go into the slot of C, so the N coordinate would be N 38° 01.202. You would then figure out the rest of the flags to discover the location of the cache. Many of these types of caches take effort to discover the coordinates.

Event Cache

Event caches are gatherings that are open to all geocachers and are orga-
nized by fellow cachers. The locations are posted by latitude and longitude.
Many times the host will also set up a few **minicaches** just for the event.
These event caches may be in various categories, including Cache In Trash
Out, meetings, and mega-events.

Cache In Trash Out (CITO) activities involve cachers meeting at a
local park or other public area and picking up litter, removing piles of junk,
and so on. Many parks will help in the efforts by supplying trash bags and
providing a way to haul off the trash collected.

Meetings are a time for fellow cachers to gather and share ideas, discuss
a variety of topics, and meet other local cachers. Some topics of discussion
might include paperless caching, what to take with you as you cache, and
different ways that people hide caches. Meals may be incorporated into a
meeting as well. The event may be held at a local restaurant or may include
a potluck at a park. This is a time for cachers to socialize and have fun.

Mega-events are specially designed to attract geocachers (more than
500 are expected to attend) on a regional, national, or international level.
Organizers must get prior approval from Groundspeak to organize this type
of event. Mega-events may be published on the geocaching.com Web site
up to a year before they occur.

Letterbox Hybrid

A **letterbox hybrid** is a mixture of letterboxing and geocaching. The
container contains the signature stamp that stays in the box (just as it
does for letterboxing), but it also conforms to the geocaching guidelines
by including a logbook. In addition, people find the container by using the
GPS (as in geocaching). The container often includes items to trade as well.

Wherigo

Wherigo is a fairly new type of geocache that allows you to use your GPS,
physical locations, and virtual objects and characters to turn geocaching
into an adventure game. Wherigo takes computer adventure games and
brings them outdoors using GPS technology so you can have a location-
based game. The first step is going to the www.wherigo.com Web site and
finding a Wherigo cartridge; these cartridges contain all the information
you need to play out a Wherigo experience. Wherigo cartridges are made
up by everyday people, and the experience can be anything from a city
walk at historical sites to a tour of a university campus—the possibilities
are endless. Wherigo operates on pocket PCs and a few GPS units such as
the Garmin Colorado or Garmin Oregon. An integration with the iPhone

is currently being looked into, but it is not yet up and running. At the current time, not many people are using the Wherigo.

Earthcache

An **earthcache** is an educational place that people can visit to view a unique earth feature, such as a crater, a place that has green sand, or an unusual rock formation. It is similar to a virtual cache in that there is no actual physical container. To get geocaching credit for the earthcache, you might have to take a picture at the location or e-mail the answers to some questions. All earthcaches are submitted and approved through the Geological Society of America, which can be reached through the www.earthcache.org Web site. For example, the town of Middlesboro, Kentucky, resides in a crater that was formed by a meteor hitting the earth and pushing the earth up to form mountains. To get credit for visiting the Middlesboro impact crater cache, geocachers need to have their picture taken at a specific location where the crater that was left behind can be seen (figure 4.5).

Benchmark Cache

Benchmarks are created and maintained by the National Geodetic Survey (NGS). A benchmark is a point whose position is known to a high degree

✖ Figure 4.5   The Middlesboro impact crater cache.

of accuracy and is usually marked by a metal disk (see figure 1.1 on p. 15). Various types of benchmarks exist, from reference marks to triangulation stations to **azimuth** marks. However, a benchmark can be a church spire or a radio, TV, or cell tower. The various types of benchmarks are used in the real world by land surveyors, builders, map makers, and other professionals who need to know exactly where they are (latitude, longitude, and altitude). These are located in plain sight, and more than likely, you have walked past them on your way to the store. When you find a benchmark, you must not tamper with, destroy, or take the benchmark. These are protected by law and may still be used by land surveyors, engineers, map makers, and other professionals. Be aware that benchmarks may be on private property or in dangerous locations.

Each geodetic marker has a permanent identifier that is matched to the data sheet with the marker's information; these data sheets can be found on the NGS Web site or through geocaching.com, which has a link to the data sheets. According to geocaching.com, there are currently 736,425 benchmarks in the database. The database usually has a very detailed documented history starting with when the benchmark was placed as well as any updates. A GPS is not needed to search for benchmarks, but it does help (along with knowing the history).

Grandfathered Cache

Grandfathered caches are those caches that still exist in the world of geocaching but are no longer supported by geocaching.com (i.e., the Web site is no longer accepting any new caches of these types). Some caches that fit into this category include the virtual cache, the Webcam cache, and the locationless cache (or waymark).

A virtual cache is an existing, permanent landmark with something unique about the area. To prove that they were at the location, geocachers must answer a variety of questions or must take pictures from the landmark and send them by e-mail to the cache owner. For example, as they are driving through a certain tunnel, the geocachers are required to count the number of emergency stairs and the number of overhead fans. The cachers then e-mail their answers to the cache owner (the person who submitted the cache to geocaching.com) in order to get credit for the cache.

Webcam caches are existing Web cameras that were placed by individuals or agencies to monitor various areas such as parks, schools, and businesses. Many Web cameras have public access to their images over the Internet. For a Webcam cache, the geocachers need to place themselves in front of the Web camera; they must also have a friend at a computer who can save a picture of them while they are on the Webcam. The next step is to upload the picture to geocaching.com as proof that they were at that location.

TRAIL TALE

Katherine

Sometimes when you're on the trail of a cache, you have to leave it alone because people are nearby. Once I was at St. Simons Island, Georgia, attending a friend's wedding. The next day, I tried to bag a few caches and came across one at a gazebo. As I approached the coordinates, I noticed a couple sitting at the gazebo and reading the paper, facing the area where I needed to search for the cache. I decided to head off and get a few more caches and try back later. I came back to the site about two hours later, and the couple was still sitting there. I had to leave the area and forget about getting that cache.

For a waymark or location-less cache, participants are given a subject or theme, and they must find an object that matches the subject. They then post a picture of the object as well as the latitude and longitude of its location. These caches are now hosted on the www.waymarking.com Web site. An example of the directions for this type of cache could be as follows: Locate statues of U.S. presidents. After finding a statue, you would log your find with the latitude and longitude and a picture of the statue. In most cases, if someone has already logged that object, then no one else can claim the same one.

Finding and Logging a Cache

Now that you have learned about the various types of caches, you are ready to go on your adventure of geocaching. Here is your step-by-step guide for how to get started in geocaching. More than likely, you will soon discover that there is a cache placed near your house, school, or place of business that you did not know was there. Depending on where you live, you likely pass by several caches on your drive to the grocery store. Let's start your adventure into this new world.

1. Register for a free account at www.geocaching.com. Come up with a geocaching name (an alias) that you will use when signing the logs. The name should be something that you will remember and something that you want to be called in the geocaching world.

2. Click on Hide & Seek a Cache. This takes you to a page that enables you to look up caches in a variety of ways.

3. For an easy way to get started near your house, enter your postal code in the Seek a Cache area of the Web page. Then hit Go. A list of caches will appear.

4. Choose any geocache from the list and click on its name.

5. Enter the latitude and longitude into your GPS or download the information using one of the methods described in chapter 2. You will normally put in several caches at a time so that you can find several on your trip. Make sure the batteries are charged in your GPS, get your bag or backpack, and head out the door.

6. When you head out into the woods caching, set a mark on your GPS to identify where your car is located. This is a good idea because if you get turned around in the woods, you will be able to find your way back. You may think this will never happen to you; however, as you are following your GPS unit, you may not pay as close attention to your surroundings as you normally would when just out for a walk.

7. As you search for the cache, you want to follow the arrows on your GPS unit. As you reach the point where your GPS indicates that you are as close to the hidden cache as possible, you should start looking. Think about the type of container you are searching for, and use your common sense and observation techniques to spot where the cache might be hiding. If you are hunting for an ammo box, then you do not need to look in tiny places—think bigger. If you are looking for a 35-millimeter film canister, then you need to look for a smaller place. If needed, decode the hint that is given on the cache page (if one is given); this can help you get closer to the cache. However, remember that these hints can be tricky. For example, the hint might be "Going up," and you might be thinking this means up in a tree or above your head when it really means you should be looking for a wooden wheelchair ramp that is "going up."

8. When you find the cache, sign and date the logbook and then return the cache to its original location. Remember, you must not take the cache container. If you have other caches to find, go and find those and then go back to your computer.

9. Log into the geocaching.com Web site and go to the cache page for the cache that you found. Go to the Navigation area on the right-hand side of the cache page and click on Log Your Visit. In the Type of Log drop-down box, select Found It. Make sure the date is correct, and write any comments you have about the experience of finding the cache. For example, you may want to say something about what happened to you on the way to the cache, such as "While I was there, I spotted four deer. What a nice place. Thanks for the hide." With this comment, you have not given away anything about the location of the cache or information about the cache, but the comment describes your unique experience of the hunt. After writing your comments, click on Submit Log Entry.

Multiple Caches on a Page

To help save paper, you can print information for multiple caches on one page. To do this, go to the cache page for a selected cache and click on No Logs under the Print heading (but do not click print yet). Copy and paste the cache information from this page into a Word document, then go to the next cache you want to find and do the same thing. You now have two caches in a Word document. You can do this with all of the caches and have several on one page. Depending on the length of the explanations for the caches, you might be able to fit five or six on one page.

Items to Take With You

This section provides some suggestions regarding what items you may or may not want to take with you as you head out on your caching adventures. Pick items from the list and add to the list as you like. What you take with you will depend on how long or where you plan on being out caching. Of course, you need your GPS unit and the list of caches that you are searching for that day.

All geocachers need some sort of bag or pack to take with them as they cache, and several things should be in the bag and in working order. Many people purchase a geocaching patch (available from Groundspeak) that they sew or iron onto their bag. This helps identify them as being a geocacher to other cachers or possibly law enforcement. The bag should include the following items:

✖ A printed copy of the Frequently Asked Questions About Geocaching provided in the Resources section of the geo-caching.com Web site. If someone asks what you are doing while you are out geocaching, you can use this sheet to explain geocaching, or you can let the person read it. These simple sheets of paper have kept many geocachers from getting in trouble.

✖ Extra pens and pencils. Remember that many of the microcaches do not have room for a writing instrument.

✖ Multiple items to trade. You will want to have these for when you come across a big enough cache or see something that you would like to trade for.

✖ A flashlight so you can look into that hole *before* sticking your hand down.

✖ Charged-up spare batteries to put in your GPS (just in case your batteries go out when you are in the middle of the woods or the middle of your hunt).

✖ An emergency poncho in case there is an unexpected rain shower.

✖ A small first aid kit that includes Band-Aids, a small roll of tape, handy wipes to keep your hands clean, and so on.

✖ A 35-millimeter film canister that contains a plastic bag stuffed inside so that you can bring out any trash that you may find along the way.

✖ Food (granola bars, fruit, snack-type food) and water. These are always good to have on hand so you can have that extra energy boost.

Your choice of clothing for geocaching is important because you need to be comfortable. It is a good idea to layer clothing in the winter and to carry a light wind jacket in the summer. Your shoes should be sturdy and comfortable. You may not think that you are going to walk much, but you ultimately do walk quite a bit. A walking stick or trekking poles are also useful, especially if the terrain is uneven. You can also use these items to poke down in holes before reaching your hand down there.

You should bring a fully charged cell phone in case you need help. This will only work if you have cell phone coverage where you are headed. In some places, the coverage may be spotty or there may be no coverage at all.

A digital or phone camera is always good to have with you so you can take pictures of some of the things you see while geocaching. For some

Paperless Caching

Many cachers have now gone paperless. They download the cache page from geocaching.com in a PDF form, upload this to a personal data assistant (PDA), and pull the information up as they go. A helpful hint when using this method is to call the cache by name when you save the PDF file to your PDA. As you save the PDF from the Web site, it usually defaults to the waypoint name. For example, the Big Tex cache would default to GCTV81. Saving caches by name ensures that they are called the same thing in both places (GPS and PDA), which makes it easier to find the information about a certain cache on your PDA.

caches, you are asked to take a picture of yourself at the cache site and to post the picture on the cache page.

One final thing you may want to bring along is a friend. It is always fun to go geocaching with another person. Hunting caches is a great way to spend some quality time with a person.

Conclusion

This chapter has given you an idea about the various types of caches, including traditional, multistage, letterbox hybrid, Wherigo, earthcache, benchmark, and other types that are out in the world. You have also learned the steps involved in looking up a cache, searching for a cache, and logging your find. You are now ready to get out there and enjoy the adventure. Remember, just when you think you have seen every type of cache, someone will put out a different type that will challenge your way of thinking. As you find more and more caches, you will start to think like a cacher, and the process will not be as difficult. We'll see you out and about.

Implementing Geocaching in Schools and Communities

After learning about geocaching and experiencing the thrill of finding caches in the world around you, you begin to open up your mind to the many possibilities that geocaching offers in school and community settings. Part II of this book is about practical applications of geocaching in classroom, physical education, and recreation environments. In the classroom, teachers can use geocaching to enhance cross-curricular learning in the areas of language arts, mathematics, science, and social studies. This can be accomplished with young students as well as with older students. In physical education, geocaching can be used to enhance health-related physical fitness experiences. There are many opportunities to use geocaching in recreational settings with families, youth organizations, and church or Scouting groups. In all instances, geocaching can be used to promote ecological and environmental education and a sense of stewardship of the earth.

Chapter 5 addresses how geocaching can be used to promote health-related fitness in physical education and other physical activity settings. It addresses the use of geocaching to encourage people to be more active, including family, friends, and groups in community or recreational settings. This chapter also covers the use of technology such as pedometers and heart rate monitors to record exercise duration and intensity while geocaching.

Chapters 6 and 7 include interdisciplinary learning experiences for beginners as well as for older students. Each chapter includes two learning experiences in each of these disciplines: language arts, mathematics, science, and social studies. Each complete learning experience includes a ready-to-use lesson containing all the components necessary for getting started. The information for each learning experience is presented in the following format:

✖ **Name.** The name of the learning experience.

✖ **Content area.** The specific content area or skills covered in the learning experience.

✖ **Appropriate age group.** Because this book will be used in school, home, and community or recreational settings—and because it will be used in countries other than the United States—appropriate age groups rather than grade levels are specified for the learning experiences. In general, beginning lessons are for students who are 9 to 14 years of age. The learning experiences for older students are appropriate for ages 14 through adulthood.

✖ **Overview.** The focus or highlights of the learning experience.

✖ **Objectives.** The specific skill and concept outcomes resulting from participation in this learning experience.

✖ **Equipment.** The equipment needed for completing the learning experience.

✖ **Organization.** How the students will be organized while working—individual, partner, small group, or large group.

✖ **Description.** The description of the total learning experience from beginning to end.

✖ **Assessment suggestions.** Examples of assessment instruments that can be applied during or after the learning experience.

✖ **Key points.** Important points to keep in mind when observing students' progress in the learning experience.

✖ **Variations.** Ways you can modify the organization of the students, introduce new skills or concepts, or change the level of difficulty, thus allowing all students to be challenged at their ability levels.

The final sections of chapters 6 and 7 contain additional ideas for developing learning experiences for young and older students. The brief descriptions offer additional ways you can use geocaching experiences to enhance learning in classroom, physical education, community, and recreation settings. These sample learning experiences are intended to give you a starting point for developing your own complete learning experiences. This section provides a broad range of ideas that instructors can select from based on their background, level of expertise, and available equipment and facilities.

The final chapter of the book, chapter 8, provides information on developing a geocaching program in a variety of situations. Because starting a geocaching program can be somewhat expensive at the outset, ideas are presented about how to write grant proposals to agencies that may provide start-up money. The chapter goes on to discuss how elementary and secondary schools may cooperate in a geocaching program, how geocaching might be conducted as an after-school program, and how geocaching might be conducted in park and recreation programs. The chapter concludes with information on how schools may cooperate with recreation agencies in setting up a geocaching program as well as ideas for how geocaching can be used by groups such as families, youth organizations, YMCAs, and Scouting programs.

GEOCACHING
FOR
HEALTH-RELATED
FITNESS

The thrill of the hunt involved in geocaching is often reason enough to participate in the sport; however, the physical activity associated with hunting and finding caches provides additional justification for integrating this sport into physical education classes, recess, and other classes in the school curriculum. Geocaching can vary with regard to its purpose and in the degree of physical activity required for participation. Geocaching can involve a walk of just a few feet for a park-and-grab cache or it can involve a hike of several miles for a cache that is located in the woods or along a hiking trail. Therefore, if enough caches are hunted in one trip or if a caching trip of sufficient distance is undertaken, it is easy for participants to meet the current physical activity guidelines and to accrue the benefits associated with being physically active.

Current physical activity guidelines for children and adolescents recommend 60 minutes of moderate or vigorous aerobic activity daily plus muscle-strengthening and bone-strengthening activities three days a week (U.S. Department of Health & Human Services, 2008). The benefits associated with being physically active include a decreased risk of many chronic diseases (ACSM, 2006). These include cardiovascular-related diseases such as heart disease, stroke, and hypertension and metabolic diseases such as type 2 diabetes and obesity. Other diseases such as osteoporosis, gall bladder disease, and colon and breast cancer have also been shown to be reduced as a result of physical activity. Furthermore, there is evidence of less depression and anxiety in people who are physically active compared to those who are not physically active. Although children and adolescents do not tend to suffer from most of these chronic diseases, many of these diseases are progressive in nature, and their development begins in childhood and adolescence. In light of the overwhelming evidence demonstrating the benefits of physical activity, any opportunity in the learning process that facilitates the integration of physical activity into a child's or adolescent's life should be used as often as possible. Geocaching provides this opportunity. The integration of geocaching into learning experiences at school and in community and recreation programs requires a monetary investment for the purchase of GPS units. However, the result of engaging individuals in physical activity that they find enjoyable makes the cost worthwhile.

Health-Related Fitness and Physical Activity

The geocaching.com Web site has several online mapping features to help geocachers find the best roads to take and the best places to park when searching for a cache. These features make it very simple to create caching excursions of specific distances and durations. The terrain rating for each cache uses a scale of 1 to 5 to indicate the length of the hike to the cache, the trail surface to be walked on, and the elevation changes of the hike. Coupling the mapping features with the terrain rating system for each cache makes it easy to estimate and vary the duration and intensity of a caching trip. For those geocachers who are premium members of geocaching.com, the Caches Along a Route feature can be used to download caches for a specific driving route, making it even easier to design a personalized caching trip. Depending on a person's preference, a caching trip might be made up of several short-distance caches in the city, a continuous walking trip that incorporates several city caches or several caches hidden in a park, or a long hike in the woods to find one or two caches.

TRAIL TALE

DuAnn

Want to cover some distance when you are out geocaching? The easiest way is to find a hiking area with several hidden caches and forget the trail map when you start your caching trip. On just such a trip, a friend and I set off to find a cache that was described as being about a 1-hour hike away. Without the trail map to guide us, we managed to take a trail that went up and over the mountain, then through a nice forest, rather than the intended shorter trail that skirted the base of the mountain. The result: Instead of a 1-hour hike, it ended up being a 3.5-hour hike. At least we remembered our water and had a great hike.

Additional ways to get people physically active through geocaching include participation in CITO (Cache In Trash Out) events and event caches. CITO events involve cachers meeting for the purpose of picking up and disposing of litter at a specific site; the participants will often go caching together in the cleaned-up area afterward. Event caches are organized by local geocachers for the purpose of discussing geocaching and socializing with others who share a common interest in geocaching. Again, group caching often occurs after the meeting. Geocaching competitions, similar to orienteering events, are another way to engage in geocaching. In these competitions, the objective is to follow clues in the form of latitude and longitude coordinates from one cache to another in an effort to be the first person to find the final hidden cache.

The fun of hunting for and discovering hidden treasures is often adequate motivation to encourage both children and adults to go caching. Therefore, the task of getting students physically active has already been accomplished by integrating geocaching into the school curriculum or into the recreation or community program. The challenge then becomes to incorporate the principles of health-related fitness into the fun of geocaching.

You can vary the duration, intensity, and purpose of caching trips in order to teach the health-related components of fitness. Furthermore, at the end of each caching excursion, you can reconvene the participants to discuss the objective of the caching trip and to reinforce guidelines regarding the recommended amount of exercise needed to meet current physical activity guidelines.

Aerobic Activities

The body's ability to perform dynamic, large muscle endurance exercise at moderate to high intensities is known as **cardiorespiratory fitness**. Improving cardiorespiratory fitness requires the cardiovascular, respiratory, and muscular systems to utilize greater amounts of oxygen to perform more work than normal in order to increase in function (ACSM, 2006). To develop cardiorespiratory fitness, people must perform **aerobic activity**, activity that requires oxygen use by the muscles. For children and adolescents, aerobic activity should occur at moderate or vigorous intensities for 60 minutes a day (U.S. Department of Health & Human Services, 2008). The components of an exercise bout that can be manipulated to improve cardiorespiratory fitness are frequency, intensity, time, and type of exercise (Powers & Howley, 2007).

- ✖ **Exercise frequency** is the number of days a week that a person should exercise.
- ✖ **Exercise intensity** is how hard a person should exercise, which can be determined by such things as heart rate, breathing rate, and perceived exertion.
- ✖ **Exercise time** is how many minutes a person should exercise.
- ✖ **Type of exercise** refers to the kind of exercise being performed, which determines how the body will improve in fitness. For the body to improve in cardiorespiratory fitness, the heart, lungs, and large muscles of the body (namely the legs) need to perform exercise that is rhythmic, continuous, and aerobic in nature, such as walking, jogging, and running.

Exercise frequency includes not only formal physical education but also recess times during and after school in both organized sport and recreational play. Because of the lack of dedicated physical education time in the schools, all school-age students should be encouraged—and provided time—to engage daily in physical activities outside of physical education and recess in order to achieve the recommended amount of physical activity. Regardless of who is responsible for the activity time, geocaching can be integrated into the activity to improve cardiorespiratory fitness. The physical education teacher as well as the classroom teacher can provide geocaching experiences for the students during the regular school day. After-school programs at schools, YMCAs, and parks and recreation centers can include geocaching activities in their programming. Parents can also take their children on geocaching excursions during the week and on the weekends, thus helping to meet the daily physical activity recommendations for frequency.

Various intensities of exercise can also be explored when geocaching. For example, you can have participants vary the exercise intensity as they search for caches—they can go from walking to jogging and finally to running as they search for a series of caches, noting the speed of travel on their GPS unit from cache to cache (figure 5.1). After completing a geocaching activity, you can discuss with the participants what is deemed to be appropriate exercise intensities.

Hidden caches that participants have to locate can also contain questions about exercise intensity. The participants can rate their intensity and effort by assessing their breathing rate, heart rate, or perceived exertion. Breathing rate can be assessed on a scale of 0 to 10, with 0 being similar to breathing when sitting quietly and 10 being similar to breathing after running as fast as possible around the track for a lap. Heart rate can be assessed by having the participants (a) calculate their target heart rate before caching (see figure 5.2 for an example), (b) monitor their heart rate effort during the cache activity, and (c) compare their actual heart rate to their calculated target heart rate.

Perceived exertion can also be assessed on a scale of 0 to 10, with 0 being little to no effort and 10 being maximum effort (similar to the 0 to 10 scale used to assess breathing rate). Relatively speaking, moderately

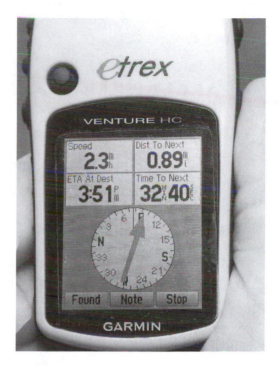

✕ **Figure 5.1** Speed of movement screen on the GPS.

Proper Exercise Intensity

Although monitoring heart rate is the most accurate method for determining appropriate exercise intensities, there are other methods. The talk test is one alternative to help participants exercise at the proper intensity while caching. With the talk test, the exercise pace is considered appropriate when the person has enough breath to talk while exercising but not enough breath to sing (www.cdc.gov/physicalactivity/everyone/measuring/index.html).

FIGURE 5.2

TARGET HEART RATE CALCULATIONS

Moderate-Intensity Range

Low end of target heart rate range: (220 − age) × 0.64

High end of target heart rate range: (220 − age) × 0.76

Vigorous-Intensity Range

Low end of target heart rate range: (220 − age) × 0.77

High end of target heart rate range: (220 − age) × 0.93

Example

Target heart rate calculation for a 12 year old:

Moderate-intensity range:

(220 − 12) × 0.64 = 133 beats per minute (low end of moderate-intensity target heart rate range)

(220 − 12) × 0.76 = 158 beats per minute (high end of moderate-intensity target heart rate range)

So a 12 year old exercising at a moderate intensity should strive to keep his or her heart rate between 133 and 158 beats per minute.

Vigorous-intensity range:

(220 − 12) × 0.77 = 160 beats per minute (low end of vigorous-intensity target heart rate range)

(220 − 12) × 0.93 = 193 beats per minute (high end of vigorous-intensity target heart rate range)

So a 12 year old exercising at a vigorous intensity should strive to keep his or her heart rate between 160 and 193 beats per minute.

intense physical activity should elicit an exertion rating of 5 or 6, while a vigorous intensity should elicit an exertion rating of 7 or 8 on a scale of 0 to 10 (U.S. Department of Health & Human Services, 2008). Upon completion of the cache series, the group can gather again for a discussion of what the participants observed about their physical effort relative to how quickly they traveled to the caches. The participants can also compare their speed of travel as determined by the GPS unit to their degree of effort on the various caches; this will enable them to see the relationship between how fast they moved and how challenging the effort felt. During the discussion, you should reinforce that moderate and vigorous intensities are required to develop and maintain cardiorespiratory fitness and its associated benefits.

The physical activity guidelines recommend 60 minutes of physical activity daily. To incorporate the concept of the proper exercise time (duration) for developing and maintaining cardiorespiratory fitness, you can create a series of multiple caches. The participants can time how long it takes them to find a single cache and return to the starting point. You can then lead a discussion about the amount of time it took the participants to travel to and from the cache and the amount of work their heart, lungs, and muscles performed on the short trip. The participants can then hunt for a series of caches that requires a longer period of time, ideally 30 to 60 minutes, to find. When the participants return to the starting point, the discussion can be resumed about the amount of effort required of the heart, lungs, and muscles for the participants to complete the longer trip compared to the shorter trip. To encourage continuous activity, you should place the caches in such a way that they are relatively easy to find. Place different items in each cache so that participants can collect the items to prove that they located all the caches. The participants can show their collected items once the series of caches has been located and the group has reconvened for discussion.

Another way to incorporate duration into geocaching would be to have numerous caches hidden in a relatively small area; participants try to find as many caches as possible in a specified time. At the end of the time period, groups could compare the number of caches they found during the time period allotted. The groups could also compare the average speed at which they traveled from one cache to the other and their overall speed of travel. This can be followed by a discussion of exercise intensity and the number of caches located by each team in the specified period of time.

Muscle-Strengthening Activities

Muscular strength is the ability of the muscles to generate maximum force, a fitness component important for performing daily tasks with ease. The exercise guideline calling for muscle-strengthening activities to be performed three days a week (U.S. Department of Health & Human Services, 2008) is easy to incorporate into geocaching. Muscle-strengthening

TRAIL TALE

Kevin

Having taught my students their introductory adapted physical activity class, I was teaching them geocaching as part of their outdoor education class when several inquired about geocaching for people with disabilities. Never wanting to miss a teachable moment, I lent them a wheelchair and had them set a series of geocaches that were easily accessible for someone using a wheelchair. We then challenged the rest of the class to go wheelchair geocaching. This was a tremendous learning experience for my students and one that I highly recommend, whatever setting you are working in. This experience not only promotes inclusion by having people think about accessible geocaching but also helps participants realize that people who use wheelchairs are perfectly capable of fully engaging in society. My students recommend raised planters as an excellent height for setting a wheelchair-accessible traditional cache. They also discovered that a 35-millimeter film canister with a strong magnet glued to it makes a great microcache that can be placed in an easily accessible location.

activities can include playlike activities such as tug-of-war; calisthenics such as push-ups, pull-ups, and crunches; and activities that require equipment such as hand weights or resistance bands. Geocaches can be set up in a station format with each cache containing different muscle-strengthening activities for the participants to perform. For example, one cache can direct participants to complete 20 crunches. Another cache can direct participants to perform 15 push-ups. Yet another cache can have a rope beside it with directions for the participants to complete a one-on-one tug-of-war match. Caches might also contain resistance bands that participants would use to perform an exercise for a specific muscle group. Another option is to set up caches that contain questions that the participants answer regarding what muscle groups are involved in different exercises. Other caches might identify a specific muscle group and require participants to determine an appropriate exercise for that muscle group. After completing the caching stations, participants can regroup and discuss their responses, the exercises they chose to complete, and the importance of muscle-strengthening exercises as part of a regular physical activity program.

Bone-Strengthening Activities

Bone strength is important for reducing the risk of bone fractures and bone loss, also known as osteoporosis, later in life. Physical activity recommendations indicate that bone-strengthening activities should be performed three days per week (U.S. Department of Health & Human Services, 2008). Bone-strengthening activities require impact with the ground, so any aerobic activity that involves jogging or running and any types of jumping activities would be appropriate. Once again, the station idea would work well for creating a series of caches specifically focused on bone strengthening. Having participants jog or run from cache to cache would be one way to combine aerobic and bone-strengthening activity. In addition, individual bone-strengthening caches could be created to meet this exercise recommendation. A cache could contain instructions for the participants to hop on one foot and then the other for a specific number of times. Another cache might instruct the participants to hop on two feet forward to a specific point (such as a tree) and then hop back to the cache. Participants could be instructed to hop backward a certain number of hops. With this type of cache, make sure that the area where the cache is located is flat and free of obstacles on the ground to reduce the

TRAIL TALE

DuAnn

Does geocaching encourage exercise? For those people who like to play with technology while they play outside, maybe it does. One study examined this question by making GPS units available to college students to check out from the recreation center for use in finding caches hidden on the college campus (Magyari & Meyer, 2009). In the first 30 days of the program, 41 students utilized the GPS check-out program and walked an average of 886 steps, slightly less than 0.5 miles, to find a cache hidden close by on campus. Within two weeks, 8 of those 41 students returned to check out a GPS unit for a second caching trip. In the second caching trip, the college students walked an average of 8,012 steps, or about 4 miles, in their search for a second cache that had also been hidden on campus. Surprised at the number of steps taken and the distance covered during the second caching activity? So were many of the students, although they felt like they had not walked that much!

risk of participants tripping and falling. A cache might contain a rope and a stopwatch, and the participants could be instructed to take turns jumping rope and timing how long each person is able to perform consecutive jumps. A cache might also contain a measuring tape and instructions for participants to measure how far forward they could jump from a standing position. Caches could even contain instructions indicating how the participants need to travel to the next cache, such as by hopping on one foot, jumping with two feet, skipping, galloping, and so on.

After completing the caches, the participants could discuss why strong bones are important and how these activities help make bones strong. They could also discuss which caches were the most difficult to perform, the easiest to perform, and the most fun to perform. The participants could also be assigned the task of creating their own bone-strengthening activity for a cache; the resulting caches can be used for a subsequent group caching activity.

Geocaching With Pedometers and Heart Rate Monitors

Many people become so involved in the fun of geocaching that they often do not realize the amount of physical activity involved in finding caches. Several methods can be used to quantify the amount of physical activity performed while caching. Many GPS units calculate the distance traveled (figure 5.3). To use this function accurately, the user needs to remember to clear the distance traveled at the beginning of the caching excursion and to note the distance traveled once the caching trip is complete.

Other ways to quantify the amount of physical activity involved in caching include the use of pedometers and heart rate monitors. Pedometers are used to determine the number of steps a person takes; a common goal is 10,000 steps daily for adults (Shape Up America!, 2009) and slightly higher step counts for children ages 6 to 12 years (Tudor-Locke et al., 2004). One idea for pedometer use would be to have participants wear pedometers while participating in both geocaching and non-geocaching activities (figure 5.4). The participants can record the number of steps taken in each type of activity, then compare and discuss differences in the number of steps taken. You can also give participants a step goal and challenge them to achieve that number of steps during the activity. Participants could compete to see who takes the most steps, or teams can be formed for competitions to see which team takes the most steps while geocaching. Discuss with participants how differences in stride length, possibly due to differences in leg length,

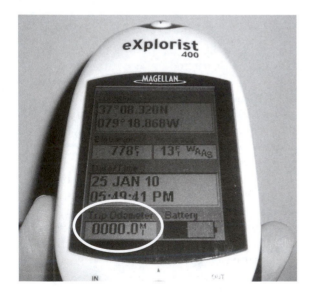

✘ **Figure 5.3** Many GPS units have an odometer (circled) to keep track of your distance traveled.

will affect the number of steps taken, even when everyone travels the same distance.

Likewise, participants can calculate their target heart rate and wear heart rate monitors when geocaching. The participants can then see when they are exercising in their target heart rate zone while caching. When traveling from one cache to another, they can try to maintain a specific exercise intensity that keeps them in their target heart rate. If heart rate monitors are not available, you can teach participants how to monitor their heart rate manually; they can do this by counting the number of heartbeats in 10 seconds, then multiplying the beats counted by 6 to convert the 10-second count to beats per minute. When participants are exercising in their target heart rate zones during geocaching, you

✖ Figure 5.4 Participants can monitor their step counts by wearing pedometers on geocaching excursions.

should make sure that caches are relatively easy to find. This will allow participants to maintain their exercising intensity and therefore their heart rates throughout the caching challenge. You can instruct participants to measure their heart rate as they find each individual cache. The participants can also wear heart rate monitors or manually measure heart rate during non-geocaching activities, with comparisons to exercising heart rate while geocaching occurring afterwards. Some heart rate monitors calculate the amount of time spent at, above, and below the target heart rate. If using this type of monitor, participants can compare the amount of time spent in their target heart rate zones during the activities that involved geocaching to those that did not. Competitions between groups of participants can also be held to see which group exercised in their target heart rate zone for the longest period of time. The competition will further motivate participants to maintain their target exercise intensity.

Discuss with participants how those with higher fitness levels will have lower heart rate responses compared to those with lower fitness levels—

even when everyone is traveling at the same pace. Explain that a person with a higher fitness level has a stronger heart that can pump more blood every time it beats and to get a strong heart, exercise in the target heart rate is necessary.

You should also encourage participants to exercise at appropriate intensities at home. If possible, set up a system to loan pedometers or heart rate monitors to participants. The participants can then involve their family in geocaching and use the pedometers or heart rate monitors to measure the family's effort on these geocaching trips. With everyone in the family wearing pedometers, students can predict who they think will take the most steps when caching. The student can then compare the number of steps taken by the various family members after the caching trip. With heart rate monitors, family members can predict who will have the highest and lowest heart rate responses and then compare their caching heart rates to one another.

Conclusion

Whether the participant is in physical education classes, at recess, in after-school activities, or with the family, health-related fitness—cardiorespiratory fitness, muscle strength, and bone strength—is integral to successful geocaching and will be incorporated naturally as a result of participation. However, with proper planning and adequate ideas for implementation, the concepts of frequency, intensity, time, and type of activity to improve these health-related components of fitness can readily become the focus of a geocaching activity. People must understand these concepts in order to develop the health-related components of fitness. By creatively combining a series of caches, you can incorporate cardiorespiratory fitness, muscle strength, and bone strength into a single caching activity. This series of caches should require the participants to complete specific tasks at each cache and to travel from cache to cache at a moderate to vigorous intensity. Whatever setting you are in and however you choose to integrate fitness into geocaching and geocaching into fitness, always make sure that the participants have fun and enjoy the thrill of the hunt!

BEGINNING EXPERIENCES WITH GEOCACHING

Part I of this book introduced the technological aspects of geocaching and provided background information on the history, values, and benefits of becoming a cacher. Beginning in chapter 5, the focus shifted to practical educational aspects of including geocaching in school and community programs. Chapter 5 focused on using geocaching to pursue a more active, healthy lifestyle.

We now shift our attention to practical applications of geocaching in classroom, community, and recreational settings. Chapter 6 includes two complete learning experiences in each of the following areas: language arts, mathematics, science, and social studies. It also includes suggested ideas for additional learning experiences. The beginning experiences with geocaching are designed to be appropriate for 9- to 14-year-old students.

Integration

To decide how to integrate geocaching experiences within classroom or instructional settings, one must investigate the scope and sequence of curricular programs across the spectrum of disciplines. The language arts are an integral part of education for young students. The language arts are the means through which a person is able to receive or decode information, think logically, and express or encode ideas through speech, writing, and nonverbal communication. According to the *National Standards for the English Language Arts* (National Council of Teachers of English and International Reading Association, 1996), as well as selected state curriculum guides, language arts can be divided into the categories of reading, writing, speaking, listening, and viewing. Subcategories include vocabulary, comprehension, composition, mechanics, questioning and answering, oral presentations, group discussions, oral directions, note taking, critical listening, personal interactions, print media, and electronic media.

The *Principles and Standards for School Mathematics* (National Council of Teachers of Mathematics, 2000)—along with several mathematics textbook series and mathematics projects such as the School Mathematics Study Group—indicate that certain mathematics concepts are taught to beginning learners through the early teen years. These topics include numbers, measurement, geometry, patterns and functions, probability and statistics, logic, and algebra.

Although not all scientists approach their subject in the same way, Gega (1994) and other science educators agree that certain steps or processes are fundamental and are invariably employed by scientists at one time or another. These processes include observing, classifying, measuring, inferring, predicting, communicating, and experimenting. The ability to perform these processes is also important for any good geocacher.

In the process of gathering information for geocaching lessons related to science, we reviewed the *National Science Education Standards* (National Research Council, 1996), several science textbook series, and projects of leading science organizations such as the American Association for the

Advancement of Science. We found that science concepts were based on and taught through units in the biological and life sciences, earth and space sciences, and physical sciences. Concepts that are particularly appropriate for geocaching experiences include the human body, the plant and animal kingdoms, life cycles, the environment and our changing earth, conservation, weather, energy, observing, and measuring.

Unlike other curricular disciplines, the social studies comprise a number of different disciplines. These include history, geography, civics, economics, sociology, anthropology, political science, and philosophy. After reviewing the *Curriculum Standards for Social Studies* (National Council for Social Studies, 1994) and several social studies textbook series, we decided that learning experiences in the areas of history and geography would be most appropriate for geocaching.

Learning Experiences

This chapter presents eight complete learning experiences (see table 6.1). Two lessons are provided from each of the four subject areas—language arts, mathematics, science, and social studies. For each learning experience, the following information is included: name, content area, appropriate age level, objectives, equipment, organization, complete description of the lesson, and assessment suggestions. In addition, tips on what to look for in student responses and suggestions for how you can modify the lesson are provided.

Table 6.1

BEGINNING LEARNING EXPERIENCES WITH GEOCACHING

Discipline and skill concept	Name	Appropriate age level
LANGUAGE ARTS		
Reading and writing: practice exchanging messages with other cachers on the Internet	Have Bug Will Travel	10- to 13-year-olds
Decrypting and encrypting messages	Alphabet Soup	9- to 12-year-olds
MATHEMATICS		
Numbers and math operations	It All Adds Up	10- to 13-year-olds
Adding, subtracting, multiplying, and dividing	A Calculated Search	9- to 12-year-olds
SCIENCE		
Biological sciences—tree identification	Forest From the Trees	10- to 12-year-olds
Earth sciences—features of the earth	Rock This	11- to 14-year-olds
SOCIAL STUDIES		
History—local and state history	I Didn't Know That!	9- to 12-year-olds
Geography—use of a map and compass	Where in the World?	9- to 12-year-olds

Language Arts 1

Have Bug Will Travel

CONTENT AREA
Gaining practice in reading and writing by exchanging messages with fellow geocachers concerning the adventures of travel bugs

APPROPRIATE AGE GROUP
10- to 13-year-olds

OVERVIEW
Students will purchase and activate a travel bug and will track the bug as it moves on its adventure from school to school or community to community.

OBJECTIVES
By participating in this learning experience, students will improve their ability to do the following:

- ✘ Read messages from geocachers who take and place their travel bug at selected sites.
- ✘ Write messages to geocachers who have moved their travel bug from one place to another.
- ✘ Use the computer and other technology to enhance their language arts skills.

EQUIPMENT
A travel bug, digital camera, paper, 3 x 5 index card, pen or pencil, and computer

ORGANIZATION
In the beginning phase of this learning experience, students will work together as a whole class or in small groups of three to five students. Once the travel bug or bugs are placed, students may work more individually when checking for travel bug movement. Each time the travel bug is moved, an individual student can be responsible for reading the message on the computer, viewing (and downloading) any digital picture submitted, writing a return message thanking the geocachers for moving the travel bug, and reporting to the class regarding the travel bug's new location.

DESCRIPTION
The beginning of this learning experience can be designated as a whole-class or small-group activity. This depends on how much you want the students to participate and how many travel bugs you are willing or able to purchase. (One suggestion is to purchase travel bugs using school or PTO funds or to do a small fund-raiser. Currently, single travel bugs cost $5.99. Four to seven travel bugs cost $5.00 each. Eight or more travel bugs cost $4.25 each.) In addition to purchasing the travel bugs, it would be good to include a small toy (stuffed animal, caricature from movie promotion, school pencil/eraser/mascot) to attach to each travel bug created.

Teach the students how they can go online to groundspeak.com to order one or more travel bugs. Next, go to geocaching.com and click on Trackables (on the left side of the page) and then click on Travel Bug FAQ (frequently asked questions). Discuss with the students all of the information provided about travel bugs and tell them about your intended project. The goal for the class is to purchase one or more travel bugs, send them on a mission such as visiting schools around the United States, and correspond with cachers who find the bugs.

Once the travel bugs are purchased, students need to go to part 2 (owner questions) on the Travel Bug FAQ page of the Web site to learn how to activate their travel bug. They will need to use the activation wizard on the Web site and the activation codes provided on the travel bugs. Make sure you develop a small note or description of your travel bug and its desired goal. You could take a digital picture of the travel bug and write about your goal of having the bug visit different schools. Mention that the goal includes having the bug get its picture taken with cachers at school sites before being relocated to a new cache nearby. Put this information on a three-by-five-inch index card (using both sides if necessary), laminate the card, and attach it to the key chain provided with the travel bug. Include a request for cachers who find your travel bug to send you their picture over the Internet, which they can do when they register the find. (Once the travel bug is registered, it will have a special code assigned to it. Anyone who finds the travel bug in a cache as it travels can use the information to contact the owners of the cache.) In addition to requesting a picture, you should ask the cachers to send the coordinates for the new location of the travel bug and any information about the school or area where they placed the bug.

Now the adventure begins. After the travel bug is activated, the next task is to place it in a nearby cache. To create a flurry of initial activity, you could ask several students to grab the travel bug on a family excursion after school or on the weekend. These students would take a picture at a local school, place the travel bug in a new location, and register the find online. You could develop a sign-up sheet for taking turns and checking out a GPS unit.

At some point, independent geocachers will grab the travel bug and take it to a location of their choice—perhaps a school in a nearby town, or, who knows, perhaps a new county or even a new state!

Now it is the students' job to take turns corresponding with the finders of the travel bug by using the Internet. Students should thank the cachers for their pictures and the messages they send. Have the students provide the cachers with some information about your school and project. Students should encourage the cachers to take the travel bug to a new school soon.

ASSESSMENT SUGGESTIONS

Create a form for students to use when reporting to the class regarding the whereabouts of their travel bug (see figure 6.1).

FIGURE 6.1

HAVE BUG WILL TRAVEL

1. Where is the travel bug located?

2. What school or area did it visit? Was the travel bug at a recreation area or a park?

3. What was the type of school? Public or private? Elementary, middle, or high school? What type of recreational or park facility did the travel bug visit (e.g., city, county, state, YMCA, church camp)?

4. How far did the bug travel?

5. What did you find out about the school/recreation/park area? If visitors do not provide you with information, do a Google search or Google Earth search.

6. Did the cachers provide a picture? If so, show it to the class.

From J.K. Taylor, D. Kremer, K. Pebworth, and P. Werner, 2010, *Geocaching for schools and communities* (Champaign, IL: Human Kinetics).

KEY POINTS

✘ Monitor the travel bug regularly to keep interest high among the participating students. Has the travel bug moved in the last week? Where has it gone? How far did it travel? What school or location did it visit? What did you learn about that school or area?

✘ When it is a given student's turn to track the travel bug, make sure that the student knows how to access the location of the bug on the computer and how to correspond with the visitors via e-mail.

VARIATIONS

✘ Create and place a travel bug with a goal of visiting different playground and recreational sites. Have cachers take pictures of themselves or their family engaged in physical activity. When cachers report placement of the travel bug in a new location, have them provide information about what types of physical activity they engage in at the parks and recreation sites. What are the most popular types of physical activity (e.g., walking, biking, swinging, jungle gym) at the site? Ask the cachers how they get to the caches and the parks or recreational sites? Do they arrive by car, walk (hike), bicycle, or in-line skate?

✘ Create and place a travel bug with a goal of visiting different historical sites and having its picture taken at these sites. Students can correspond with geocachers who take and place the travel bug as well as research information about the history of a given site.

✘ Create and place a travel bug with a goal of visiting state capitals or county seats and having its picture taken at these sites. If you start this project at the beginning of a school year, you can track how many states or county sites are visited during the school year. Students can correspond with geocachers who take and place the travel bug as well as research information about each state capital or county seat.

Language Arts 2

Alphabet Soup

CONTENT AREA

Reading and writing using a coding system to decrypt and encrypt messages

APPROPRIATE AGE GROUP

9- to 12-year-olds

OVERVIEW

Students will decrypt and encrypt real cache messages that provide helpful hints about the location of a cache.

OBJECTIVES

By participating in this learning experience, students will improve their ability to do the following:

✘ Use the alphabet to decode and encode hints for finding and hiding geocaches.

✘ Work cooperatively with a partner to decode and encode hints.

✘ Use a computer to locate several geocaches of interest and decode the hints that provide clues about where the caches are hidden.

✘ Use a GPS unit and a decrypted hint to locate a geocache.

EQUIPMENT

A computer, several GPS units, paper, and pens or pencils

ORGANIZATION

This learning experience will begin with the students together as a whole class and with you guiding the instruction. During this phase, the students will learn the process of coding and decoding messages by using the decryption system adopted by geocachers around the world. After students have learned this process, they will work in partnerships or groups of three to decode several messages from local caches as well as develop their own messages for a cache they might hide. Finally, the students will check out a GPS unit from the teacher, select a local geocache, decode the message, and go with their parents or friends after school or on a weekend to find the cache.

DESCRIPTION

As a whole-class activity, conduct a discussion with students about how code systems have been used to communicate with others. Examples might include the development of Morse code for transmitting telegraph messages across the country before the telephone was invented, the use of American Indian code talkers to transmit messages during World War II, and the use of text messaging to talk to friends on cell phones.

Next, talk to the students about the use of a simple code system for providing hints about the exact location of geocaches. Using the 26 letters of the alphabet, you simply place the first 13 letters (A to M) over the second 13 letters (N to Z). Thus, A becomes N, N becomes A, B becomes O, O becomes B, and so on. This can be a useful way to provide hints to the location of a cache when geocachers are having difficulty finding its whereabouts using the latitude and longitude coordinates alone. And using a code keeps muggles from understanding what is going on.

A	B	C	D	E	F	G	H	I	J	K	L	M
N	O	P	Q	R	S	T	U	V	W	X	Y	Z

Place a few examples on the chalkboard or whiteboard and go through them with the class. For example, "haqre gur obbx" means "under the book." "Va gur qenjre" means "in the drawer."

After the students feel comfortable with the coding system, partner them up with an appropriate person. Assign them the task of logging on to a computer (in class or in the library), finding three to five local caches (using your zip code) with hints, and decoding each of the messages.

Finally, allow students to check out a GPS unit overnight or over a weekend. Have them select one or more geocaches with hints on the computer, download the description of the caches, enter the coordinates for the caches on the GPS unit, and go find the caches with a friend or their parents using the hints as extra clues to pinpoint the cache. Students should report back to the class on their experience and success in finding the cache.

ASSESSMENT SUGGESTIONS

Provide each student with a practice decoding sheet similar to the one shown in figure 6.2. Have students decrypt each hint and check their answers for correctness. Answers are as follows:

1. no really on the ground under some ivy
2. rock face and two small pines
3. Kneel down on top of the oil pan and reach toward the fan. Cache is hanging from where the radiator once sat.
4. base of plant on downward slope
5. in the tree above the pine log you will see

KEY POINTS

✖ When decoding and encoding hints using the geocaching system, make sure that the first 13 letters of the alphabet are directly over the last 13 letters so that the messages are accurate.

✖ Remember that hints are to be just that. They should not tell a geocacher exactly where a cache is located. They should just provide a clue.

VARIATIONS

✖ As an in-class practice session, have the students write their spelling words for the week, a sentence, or a short paragraph using the geocaching decryption system. Allow students to share their work and decode each other's work.

✖ Have the students create a geocache of their own. This would include selecting a place to hide their cache and creating an encrypted message that provides clues to help guide geocachers in locating the cache.

FIGURE 6.2

ENCRYPTED HINTS

Name _____   Teacher _____

Use the geocaching decrypting system to translate each of the following hints:

1. ab ernyyl ba gur tebhaq haqre fbzr vil

2. ebpx snpr naq gjb fznyy cvarf

3. Xarry qbja ba gbc bs gur bvy cna naq ernpu gbjneq gur sna. Pnpur vf unatvat sebz jurer gur enqvngbe bapr fng.

4. onfr bs cynag ba qbjajneq fybcr

5. va gur gerr nobir gur cvar ybt lbh jvyy frr

Mathematics 1

It All Adds Up

CONTENT AREA
Simple mathematical operations and applying digits into latitude and longitude coordinates

APPROPRIATE AGE GROUP
10- to 13-year-olds

OVERVIEW
Students will identify a multicache near where they live that requires the use of numbers to locate the multiple stages in the process of finding the final cache destination. They will then use a GPS unit to find each stage by applying the proper numbers and solutions to each stage until they find the cache destination.

OBJECTIVES
By participating in this learning experience, students will improve their ability to do the following:

✘ Conduct an online search to find a multicache that requires the use of placing numerical digits in appropriate spaces to decipher a latitude and longitude coordinate.

✘ Use simple mathematical operations to calculate solutions to math problems.

✘ Use a GPS unit and multiple clues to find a multicache.

EQUIPMENT
A computer, a GPS unit, paper, and a pencil

ORGANIZATION
The best way to conduct this learning experience is by loaning a GPS unit to individual students and their families. Over time, all students can get a chance to complete this learning experience. After locating an appropriate multicache online using geocaching.com—and downloading the cache description as well as the beginning coordinates onto the GPS unit—the students will have their parents drive them to a location near the initial listed coordinates for the cache. From there, the students and their families will walk or hike to each of the deciphered coordinates until they find the final cache location.

DESCRIPTION
Type up a short letter to parents offering them an opportunity to go caching with their child. Have each student take the letter home. Develop a sign-up schedule for when each set of parents would like to take their child geocaching. According to the schedule, allow each student to check out a GPS unit to be used overnight or over a weekend.

Once the schedule is created, develop a list of steps or procedures that the students and their parents can follow.

1. Go online to geocaching.com. Click on Hide & Seek a Cache. Enter your postal code and perform a search. When the results are displayed, scroll down until you find a multicache in your area that involves using numbers to find several stages in the process of locating the final cache location. (Multicaches are identified by an icon of two yellow bricks on the left of the page.) Select that cache.

2. Download a printout of the cache description.

3. Download the initial cache coordinates onto the GPS unit.

4. Travel to the location of the initial cache coordinates.

5. Use the numbers at the initial cache coordinates to solve or answer the mathematics problem provided (see figure 6.3). (Numbers may be taken from a date, dedication, number of columns, stars, figures, and so on, at the location.) Place the appropriate digits in the proper order to find the next set of coordinates. Proceed to the next cache coordinates by driving, biking, or walking.

6. Repeat step 5 until the final cache is found. Sign and date the log inside the final cache to indicate your discovery.

7. When you return home, go online and log the cache by opening the cache page and sending a message to the owner of the cache. The message should indicate that you found the cache and should describe the experience. The message should also thank the owner for the hide.

8. Print out a copy of your message to the owner of the cache. Take a copy of the message to school to receive credit for completing the experience.

9. Return the GPS unit to school, and bring a copy of the log of the cache.

Develop a certificate to be awarded to each student for completing the cache experience.

ASSESSMENT SUGGESTIONS

Have the students register their visit to the multicache on the geocaching.com Web site. Have them print a copy of their solution for each of the stages to the cache as well as the message that they send to the owners of the cache.

KEY POINTS

✘ For a multicache involving numbers, digits are often given a place value such as second or third digit. In these instances, teach the students that it means they should read the number from left to right (not units, tens, hundreds, thousands). For example, with the number 1954, 9 is the second digit, and 5 is the third digit.

✘ Have parents or adult leaders check the work of the students as they progress through the multicache. Placing numbers in the wrong places will only lead to going to incorrect coordinates, finding nothing, and getting lost.

FIGURE 6.3

EXAMPLE OF A MULTICACHE INVOLVING MATHEMATICS

London Trails

Initial coordinates: N 43° 03.015, W 089° 00.710

Stage 1: The coordinates listed are for the starting place. Drive, hike, or bike to these coordinates located at a place called London Bridges. Find the year on the building of London Bridges (1924). Substitute the numbers from the date found into the following coordinates: N 43° 0c.b5b, W 089° 00.6bd. The numbers in the date correspond to abcd. For example, replace each b with a 9, and replace each d with a 4. Disregard the fact that a 9 already exists in the remainder of the coordinates. After plugging in the numbers, proceed to those coordinates.

Stage 2: When you arrive at the next location, you will find two joined stars. In the next set of coordinates, the symbol * represents the number of points per star, or the total number of points divided by two (16 ÷ 2 = 8). Replace the * in the following coordinates with the solution to the division problem: N 43° 02.893, W 089° 00.7*9. Then proceed to those coordinates.

Stage 3: At this location, you must seek a concrete structure near ground level that has a year on it (1905). The numbers in the date will correspond to efgh. You will only use the letter g (e, f, and h are distracters). Substitute the numbers in the date into these coordinates: N 43° 02.8gg, W 089° 0g.845. Then proceed to those coordinates.

Stage 4: At this location, you will find the final cache.

From J.K. Taylor, D. Kremer, K. Pebworth, and P. Werner, 2010, *Geocaching for schools and communities* (Champaign, IL: Human Kinetics).

VARIATIONS

✖ Organize a group of students who will accompany you or a volunteer parent to find a multicache as an after-school or weekend experience.

✖ Using numbers on local landmarks (e.g., year the school was built, address on a nearby building, number on a fire hydrant, telephone number on a sign), have the students develop and register a new multicache online for others to find. This may be a group project or a project for the whole class.

Mathematics 2

A Calculated Search

CONTENT AREA

Operations—adding, subtracting, multiplying, dividing

APPROPRIATE AGE GROUP

9- to 12-year-olds

OVERVIEW

Students will learn to solve problems in a mathematics unit of study in the classroom. Then, as a motivational technique, they will use a GPS unit to find and solve sample math problems at caches placed around the school or at a community park.

OBJECTIVES

By participating in this learning experience, students will improve their ability to do the following:

✖ Correctly answer questions related to mathematics problems appropriate for their age level.

✖ Use a GPS unit to locate latitude and longitude coordinates.

✖ Work independently or cooperate with a partner or small group.

EQUIPMENT

One or more GPS units, paper to be used for calculations, clipboards, pencils, and several plastic containers to be used for hiding math problems

ORGANIZATION

Students will begin this learning experience in the classroom with the whole class in a selected unit of instruction on operations in mathematics. Use the mathematics textbook and provide proper instruction to students about how to successfully solve selected mathematics problems. Then, to gain practice in solving mathematics problems, students will individually or in partners or small groups go outside to locate hidden caches you have placed on the school grounds; these caches contain selected mathematics problems appropriate to the unit of instruction. Students may be given the time to locate the caches during class time, before or after school, or during recess under the supervision of the teacher or a parent volunteer.

DESCRIPTION

This learning experience can be conducted during any unit on mathematics. Conduct the class instruction as normal. Teach the whole class the new mathematics concepts. Then, you can bring geocaching into the unit in order to serve as a motivational technique, to provide a novel learning experience, and to integrate the use of technology in mathematics. Write several mathematics problems down on small sheets of paper and place one in each of the cache containers. Take the cache containers out onto the school grounds and use a GPS unit to mark the location of each cache as you hide them in appropriate places. Next, download all of the coordinates onto each of the GPS units you plan to use. Develop an answer sheet that students can use to enter their answers as they complete the experience.

Take the students outside. This activity may be done individually, in partnerships, or as a whole-class activity. As the teacher, you may supervise the experience or get a parent volunteer to supervise the experience. Students will locate one of the assigned caches, solve the mathematics problem on notebook paper, write their answer on the answer sheet provided, and proceed to each of the remaining caches to solve each of the problems. When all of the caches have been found and all of the mathematics problems solved, the answers will be checked for correctness.

ASSESSMENT SUGGESTIONS

Develop an answer sheet with an identified space to place each answer (see figure 6.4). Develop a separate answer sheet with a key that provides the answers to each of the problems. This way, the students can check their own answers, a parent volunteer can check the answers, or the teacher can check the answers. Answers to the mathematics problems in figure 6.4 are as follows:

1. 14,575
2. 3,289
3. 7/16
4. 93,018
5. 289.154
6. 21
7. 9
8. The total cost of groceries is $22.53; the tax is $1.35; the total bill is $23.88; the change is $6.12.

KEY POINTS

✖ Before sending the students outside to locate the caches, make sure that they are confident in their ability to solve the mathematics problems. If necessary, group strong students with others who are less sure of their success.

✖ Observe the students while they are outside using the GPS units to find the caches. If a person or group seems to be confused or is having problems operating the GPS unit, provide those students with the help they need.

FIGURE 6.4

SAMPLE ANSWER SHEET WITH MULTIPLE TYPES OF TYPICAL MATHEMATICS PROBLEMS

Name _____   Teacher _____

A Calculated Search

1. 1,944 + 2,875 + 9,756 =

2. 4,247 − 958 =

3. 1/4 + 3/8 − 3/16 =

4. 2,514 × 37 =

5. 3,759 ÷ 13 =

6. 3(5 − 2 + 4) =

7. 3(x − 5) = 12. Solve for x.

8. Monica is sent to the grocery store by her mother with $30.00. She buys 3 pounds of apples for $1.29 per pound. She also buys a box of cereal for $3.58, two cans of tuna for $2.56 each, a gallon of milk for $3.69, 1/2 pound of lunch meat that sells for $6.58 per pound, and a loaf of bread for $2.98. The tax on the groceries is 6%. What is the total cost of the groceries, the tax, and the total bill? How much change will Monica have to return to her mother?

From J.K. Taylor, D. Kremer, K. Pebworth, and P. Werner, 2010, *Geocaching for schools and communities* (Champaign, IL: Human Kinetics).

VARIATIONS

✖ Select a different unit of mathematics instruction such as one using fractions, geometry, estimation and prediction, word problems, or beginning algebra. Put problems from this unit in the caches.

✖ Have students from one class make up some mathematics problems from their current unit of instruction and hide them in caches. Then, have students from another class locate the problems with the GPS units and solve the problems.

Science 1

Forest From the Trees

CONTENT AREA
Biological life sciences—identification of trees

APPROPRIATE AGE GROUP
10- to 12-year-olds

OVERVIEW
Students will learn how to identify trees in a classroom setting (in a school, community center, or park and recreation facility). They will then use a GPS to navigate to selected coordinates that lead them to specific trees on the school grounds or park area. Next, they will practice identifying the trees they have found.

OBJECTIVES
By participating in this learning experience, students will improve their ability to do the following:

✖ Identify trees that are natural to the place where they live.

✖ Get clues to the identification of a tree from the tree type, leaf, bark, fruit, twig, or form.

✖ Learn both the scientific and common name for each of the trees.

✖ Work cooperatively with a small group to complete the tree identification assignment.

✖ Properly use a computer to access information about the process of identifying trees.

✖ Properly use a GPS unit to locate latitude and longitude coordinates that will enable them to find specific assigned trees.

EQUIPMENT
One or more computers, GPS units (1 to 10), a tree identification guide (use figure 6.5 or your own field guide to trees, such as Petrides, Petrides, & Peterson [1998] or Petrides, Wehr, & Peterson [1998]), a list of coordinates to guide

students to specific sites, worksheets for each group, pencils, and an answer sheet with the correct answers for this learning experience

ORGANIZATION

The assignment will start in the classroom with whole-class instruction. Students will use their science texts or field guides to the identification of trees to begin learning that trees can be identified by analyzing them according to a combination of clues—type, leaf, bark, fruit, twig, or form. Next, students will be divided into groups of three to five students. Working in groups during class time or recess, students will use the GPS units to locate the coordinates of assigned trees. While at the tree locations, the students will take a leaf and fruit sample; they will also write a description of the type, leaf, bark, twig, and form of the tree. Still working in groups, the students will take their gathered information and use the field guide or Internet sites to identify the assigned trees.

DESCRIPTION

In their late childhood or early adolescent years, students learn about the biological life sciences. These studies can include learning about trees. Using whole-class instruction, provide a definition of a tree (a woody plant with roots, a trunk, branches, and a crown on top). You could provide an analogy comparing trees to families. Each has characteristics. Family characteristics include hair color, eye color, height, weight, and so on (based on genes or DNA). Trees are characterized by leaf, bark, twig, and form. Use a field guide to trees or an appropriate Internet source. Talk to the students about identifying trees around the school or at a nearby park. Provide them with all of the information they will need to conduct their project.

Lead a discussion about why trees are so important in all of our lives. Discuss the process of photosynthesis—converting light energy into chemical energy and converting carbon dioxide and water into oxygen and carbohydrate. Discuss how trees take root and help prevent soil erosion. Discuss how we use tree products. Talk about fruit, nuts, maple syrup, lumber, furniture, baskets, paper, and so on.

Organize the students into small groups of three to five. Show students the worksheets and explain how to use them. Make sure that students know how to use the GPS units. If you have enough GPS units, you can have the whole class conduct their identification tasks simultaneously. If you have only one or two units, you can send the students out to do their field work independently. You may use class or recess time. You can ask for volunteer parents to help supervise.

The first task is to enter the latitude and longitude coordinates of the selected trees on the school or park grounds onto the GPS units. To set this experience up, you must select the trees and coordinates in advance. You should select eight trees. To enter the coordinates onto the GPS units, you can use a cable to connect the GPS units to the computer and then transfer all of the coordinates automatically. You could also have the students enter the coordinates of the trees manually if you think this would be a valuable learning experience.

Prepare a worksheet with tree identification procedures (see figure 6.5, *a* and *b*) for each tree. (Other excellent tree identification guides can be found online at www.fw.vt.edu/dendro and www.arborday.org/trees/treeguide.) Make sure that you introduce your students to a proper guide for the area where you live. For example, a tree guide for the northern states will not work for the southern or western states. The task for the students (in small groups) is to enter the data properly on the worksheet regarding the characteristics of each tree (i.e., type, leaf, bark, twig, and form).

Next, the small groups go out onto the school grounds to begin identifying each of the trees. They collect appropriate data for each tree—type of tree, leaf sample, description of bark, what a twig looks like, and the general form of the tree. Provide each group with a tree identification procedures worksheet (figure 6.5, *a* and *b*) and a plastic bag for each tree so they can collect samples. The students will fill in the answers regarding the identification of each tree as they complete the experience. Their next task is to cross-check their collected data with information on one of the Internet sites or in one of the field guides to trees. Finally, once they think that they have enough information and have cross-checked for correctness, they can fill in the answers on the answer key sheet (see figure 6.6) by writing in each of the names of the trees.

If the groups go out to the school grounds at different times, they may identify the trees in any order. If all groups go out simultaneously, a rotation schedule (figure 6.7) may be helpful to prevent groups from bunching up at one tree.

ASSESSMENT SUGGESTIONS

After the students fill out the answer sheet, check the answers of each group. You can also allow the students to check their own answers or have one group check another group's answers.

KEY POINTS

✖ Pay attention to whether students are well versed in sequentially analyzing the properties of the trees—type, leaf, bark, fruit, and so on—and that they can distinguish between **coniferous** (has needles and stays green all year) and **deciduous** (sheds its leaves each year) trees. Make sure they are not getting distracted by irrelevant clues such as the bird's nest in the tree, the plants around the tree, or the car driving by.

✖ Teach the students to appreciate and respect trees. Make sure they do not deface the trees, hang from weak branches, or tear small branches from the trunk.

✖ Make sure the environment is safe. Remove broken glass. Help the children learn to identify and avoid noxious plants such as poison ivy, poison oak, and raspberry bushes with prickly spines.

✖ Make sure the students are grouped well so that they work cooperatively and so that each person has a chance to contribute to the group process.

FIGURE 6.5a

A DICHOTOMOUS KEY TO IDENTIFY DECIDUOUS TREES

■ **Deciduous**—*tree has broad leaves*
(choose either opposite or alternate branching)

☐ **Opposite branching** (choose either compound or simple leaves)

  ☐ **Compound leaves** (choose 9 to 11 or 5 to 9 leaflets)

    ☐ 9 to 11 leaflets, leaflets do not have stems (black ash)

    ☐ 5 to 9 leaflets, leaflets have stems, smile-shaped leaf scar (white ash)

  ☐ **Simple leaves** (choose either smooth or notched leaf margins)

    ☐ Leaf margins smooth, 5 lobes (sugar maple)

    ☐ Leaf margins notched, 3-5 lobes (red maple)

☐ **Alternate branching** (choose either compound or simple leaves)

  ☐ **Compound leaves** (choose either 5 to 7 or 7 to 17 leaflets)

    ☐ Leaflets over 2 inches long, 5 to 7 hairless leaflets, egg-shaped nut (shagbark hickory)

    ☐ Leaflets over 2 inches long, 7 to 17 slightly hairy leaflets, leaf 12 to 36 inches long (black walnut)

  ☐ **Simple leaves** (choose leaves that are either lobed or not lobed)

    ☐ Leaves lobed, smooth or toothed margins (choose either pointed or rounded lobes)

      ☐ Pointed lobes, leaves hairless, sinuses no closer than 1/2 inch to mid-vein (red oak)

      ☐ Rounded lobes, even lobes and sinuses, leaves hairless (white oak)

    ☐ Leaves not lobed (choose either papery bark or nonpapery bark)

      ☐ Leaves toothed, papery bark (choose either oval or rounded leaves)

        ☐ Leaves oval and 2 to 3 inches, white peeling bark (white birch)

        ☐ Leaves with rounded heart-shaped base, 3 to 4 inches long, yellow or bronzed bark (yellow birch)

      ☐ Leaves toothed, bark not papery (choose leaf stems that are either flat or round)

        ☐ Leaf stems flat (choose a tooth-shaped leaf small, large, or triangular)

          ☐ Leaves have small, fine teeth/points/sharp edges <1/16 inch long, bark usually white (trembling aspen)

          ☐ Leaves have large teeth, bark usually white (big-toothed aspen)

          ☐ Leaf is triangular-shaped, with coarse teeth (cottonwood)

        ☐ Leaf stems round (choose either long and narrow or stems almost as wide as long)

          ☐ Leaves long and narrow (choose either 5 to 6 or 3 to 5 inches)

            ☐ 5- to 6-inch long hairy leaves, fringe on bottom of leaf, bark very dark (black cherry)

            ☐ 3- to 5-inch long leaves, smooth gray bark (American birch)

          ☐ Leaf stems almost as wide as they are long (basswood)

Based upon the characteristics I have observed, I believe this tree is a

_____

From J.K. Taylor, D. Kremer, K. Pebworth, and P. Werner, 2010, *Geocaching for schools and communities* (Champaign, IL: Human Kinetics). LEAF Program.

FIGURE 6.5b

A DICHOTOMOUS KEY TO IDENTIFY CONIFEROUS TREES

■ **Coniferous**—*tree has needles*
(choose either needles in bundles or groups or needles single or flattened and scaly)

☐ **Needles in bundles or groups** (choose either clusters or 2 to 5 per bundle)

    ☐ **Needles in clusters** (tamarack)

    ☐ **Needles 2 to 5 per bundle** (choose either 5 needles or needles in pairs)

        ☐ 5 needles per bundle (white pine)

        ☐ Needles in pairs (choose either needles 3 to 4 inches long or under 2 inches)

            ☐ Needles 3 to 4 inches long (red pine)

            ☐ Needles under 2 inches (choose either dark gray bark or orange and brown bark)

                ☐ Bark dark gray (Jack pine)

                ☐ Bark orange and brown, cones 1 to 2 1/2 inches long (Scotch pine)

☐ **Needles single or flattened and scaly** (choose square, round, or scaly needles or flat needles)

    ☐ **Needles square, round, or scaly** (choose scaly and flattened or square or round)

        ☐ Needles scaly and flattened (northern white cedar)

        ☐ Needles square or round (choose one of the following needle descriptions)

            ☐ Needles 1/3 to 3/4 inch long, twig hairless (white spruce)

            ☐ Needles 1/4 to 3/4 inch long, new twigs have hair, grows in wet areas (black spruce)

            ☐ Needles 1/4 to 3/4 inch long, droopy branches, cones 4 to 7 inches (Norway spruce)

    ☐ **Needles flat** (choose needles 1/2 inch long with stem or 3/4 to 1 1/4 inches with no stem)

        ☐ Needles 1/2 inch long, with a short stem (eastern hemlock)

        ☐ Needles 3/4 to 1 1/4 inches long, with no stem (balsam fir)

Based upon the characteristics I have observed, I believe this tree is a

_____

From J.K. Taylor, D. Kremer, K. Pebworth, and P. Werner, 2010, *Geocaching for schools and communities* (Champaign, IL: Human Kinetics). LEAF Program.

FIGURE 6.6

TREE IDENTIFICATION KEY

Tree 1 Location (latitude and longitude): N_____ W_____ Tree identity Common name: _____ Scientific name: _____	**Tree 2** Location (latitude and longitude): N_____ W_____ Tree identity Common name: _____ Scientific name: _____
Tree 3 Location (latitude and longitude): N_____ W_____ Tree identity Common name: _____ Scientific name: _____	**Tree 4** Location (latitude and longitude): N_____ W_____ Tree identity Common name: _____ Scientific name: _____
Tree 5 Location (latitude and longitude): N_____ W_____ Tree identity Common name: _____ Scientific name: _____	**Tree 6** Location (latitude and longitude): N_____ W_____ Tree identity Common name: _____ Scientific name: _____
Tree 7 Location (latitude and longitude): N_____ W_____ Tree identity Common name: _____ Scientific name: _____	**Tree 8** Location (latitude and longitude): N_____ W_____ Tree identity Common name: _____ Scientific name: _____

From J.K. Taylor, D. Kremer, K. Pebworth, and P. Werner, 2010, *Geocaching for schools and communities* (Champaign, IL: Human Kinetics).

FIGURE 6.7

ROTATION SCHEDULE

Group 1	Group 2	Group 3	Group 4	Group 5	Group 6	Group 7	Group 8
Tree 1	Tree 2	Tree 3	Tree 4	Tree 5	Tree 6	Tree 7	Tree 8
Tree 2	Tree 1	Tree 4	Tree 3	Tree 6	Tree 5	Tree 8	Tree 7
Tree 3	Tree 5	Tree 1	Tree 7	Tree 2	Tree 8	Tree 4	Tree 6
Tree 5	Tree 8	Tree 7	Tree 6	Tree 1	Tree 4	Tree 3	Tree 2
Tree 7	Tree 4	Tree 6	Tree 2	Tree 8	Tree 3	Tree 1	Tree 5
Tree 8	Tree 3	Tree 2	Tree 5	Tree 4	Tree 7	Tree 6	Tree 1
Tree 6	Tree 7	Tree 5	Tree 8	Tree 3	Tree 1	Tree 2	Tree 4
Tree 4	Tree 6	Tree 8	Tree 1	Tree 7	Tree 2	Tree 5	Tree 3

VARIATIONS

✗ Perform the same activity, but use types of flowers as GPS identification sites—rose, pansy, tulip, chrysanthemum, bird of paradise, calla lily, day lily, coneflower, and so on.

✗ Perform the same activity, but use types of shrubbery as GPS identification sites—boxwood, privet, red tip, hydrangea, rhododendron, dwarf nandina, viburnum, azalea, and so on.

✗ Perform the same activity, but use rock samples or formations as GPS identification sites—granite, sandstone, limestone, quartz, mica, feldspar, basalt, obsidian, and so on.

Science 2

Rock This

CONTENT AREA
Earth sciences—features of the earth

APPROPRIATE AGE GROUP
11- to 14-year-olds

OVERVIEW

While studying about earth sciences and the environment, students will conduct an Internet search for earthcaches near where they live. They will then go find the cache and report back to the class about what they found at the site.

OBJECTIVES

By participating in this learning experience, students will improve their ability to do the following:

✖ Learn about various geological features of the earth.

✖ Conduct an individual search on the Internet and report their findings to the class.

✖ Increase their levels of physical activity through family or group walks or bike rides during earthcaching experiences outside of school.

EQUIPMENT

A computer, paper, and a pen or pencil (if an earthcache is located near the school or community, a GPS unit will also be needed to locate the cache)

ORGANIZATION

This learning experience will begin with whole-class instruction and then proceed with individual or small-group investigations. Toward the end of the learning experience, the individuals or groups will report their findings to the whole class or share their findings with another class of students.

DESCRIPTION

During the late years of childhood and early years of adolescence, students study about the earth sciences and the environment. In this learning experience, you will initially conduct whole-class instruction to inform the students about earthcaches and the subject of geology. Students are then given an individual or group assignment to find an earthcache of interest. They might use their local area, the place where their grandparents live, a place they have gone on vacation, or a place they might like to visit. After determining their area of interest, the students will go to geocaching.com and enter the zip code, city, state, or country. They will then scroll down through the search results until they find an earthcache. An earthcache is a geological land formation—such as a glacier, continental divide, specific types of rock, river attributes, and so on—that a geocacher has developed GPS coordinates for so that others can discover the location. Students will read about the features of the earthcache, perhaps conducting a Google search as well, and report back to the whole class on their findings. In some instances, the class might take a field trip to visit the earthcache, or students may visit an earthcache with their family.

Following are four examples of earthcaches.

Example 1: Multidirectional Multiearthcache

Cache identification number: GC1693V

Latitude and longitude coordinates: N 35° 33.181, W 082° 19.625

Feature: Eastern Continental Divide

Location: Black Mountain, North Carolina

Science information: At this site, a surface hydrology (water runoff) experiment can be performed by pouring two small jugs or cans of water onto the pavement just 150 feet (46 m) apart from each other. By using a GPS unit or a compass to note the direction of the flow of water, a person learns that the water from one jug flows south and east to the Atlantic Ocean, and the water from the other jug flows southwest, north, west, and finally south into the Gulf of Mexico. Each starts out flowing into a tiny rivulet and then flows into a creek, a stream, a set of rivers, and finally out to sea. The locations where each container of water enters the ocean are 667 miles apart. The water ending up in the Atlantic Ocean travels 378 river miles. The water entering the Gulf of Mexico travels 1,848 miles.

Example 2: Creeper Karst Earthcache

Cache identification number: GC1485N

Latitude and longitude coordinates: N 36° 39.384, W 081° 54.408

Feature: Karst formations

Location: Abingdon, Virginia

Science information: Karst landscapes are formed as a result of mildly acidic water (acid rain) eroding a soluble bedrock such as limestone. The rain that falls to the earth picks up carbon dioxide in the air that dissolves into each raindrop. Once the rain droplets reach the ground, they pass through the soil, where they pick up even more carbon dioxide, resulting in a mild carbonic acid. Over time, the carbonic acid dissolves the bedrock. This creates an underground drainage system with extensive caves and caverns. Above-ground features may show ridges, vertical shafts, sinkholes, disappearing streams, and reappearing springs. There is nothing we can do to correct the erosion of the limestone, but we can work to reduce carbon emissions by living a greener life.

Karst topography is named for the kras region in Slovenia (*karst* is a German word) partially extending into Italy where it is called Carso.

In Abingdon, Virginia, the karst formation is part of the Conococheague geological formation (a bigger geological land formation) (see figure 6.8). Although some sinkholes are visible, no one knows which directions the underground creeks run.

Example 3: Glacial Drumlin Trail

Cache identification numbers: GC174ER, GC1C0AE, GCP9MH, GCXNK7, GCZKBX, GC15ZM4, GC1CCXX, GCQP07

Latitude and longitude coordinates: 14 different caches exist along the Glacial Drumlin Trail.

Features: Glacial terrain, including moraines, drumlins, and kettle lakes

✖ **Figure 6.8** Geocache of a karst formation in Abingdon, Virginia.

Location: A Rails-to-Trails path running 52 miles from Waukesha to Cottage Grove, Wisconsin

Science information: The accumulation of ice covering continental land masses is a common occurrence in the earth's history. Large sheets of ice advanced, changing the landscape by eroding bare rock and carrying materials long distances. Eventually, the glaciers melted and recessed, affecting the land by leaving behind till and blocks of ice that eventually created glacial features such as moraines, drumlins, and kettle lakes.

A moraine is a mound, ridge, or other accumulation of till deposited by direct action of glacier ice.

A drumlin is a smoothly rounded, elongated, and oval hill, mound, or ridge of compact glacial till. Built under the margin of ice, a drumlin is shaped by the glacier's flow. It usually has a blunt nose facing the direction from which the ice approached and a gentle slope tapering in the other direction.

Kettle lakes were formed where a block of ice broke off and was buried. The block of ice melted, creating the lakes.

Example 4: Cleeve Hill Earthcache

Cache identification number: GCPE04

Latitude and longitude coordinates: N 51° 56.320, W 002° 01.214

Features: Rock formations, fossils, and fault lines

Location: Cleeve Hill, near Cheltenham, England

Science information: The limestone rocks of the Cotswolds formed about 170 million years ago from deep layers of sediment settling in a shallow tropical sea. Later on, sea levels were lowered, the land surface was raised up, and the Cotswold Hills came into existence.

Cleeve Common, now a golf course, had been quarried for limestone for houses and roads for a very long time. The many small quarries reveal fascinating rock formations under the common, and the types of rocks had different uses. Smooth-grained rocks with few imperfections, such as lower freestone, made good building stone. Coarser, rubbly rocks, such as pea grit, with many fossils were suitable for roads and field walls.

Frequent earthquakes cracked the earth's crust, creating faults. The faulted rock sections shifted upward or downward, and continuity of the original beds was broken.

ASSESSMENT SUGGESTIONS

Depending on the earthcache found and studied, develop a short quiz regarding the information discovered about the geological features. Figure 6.9 is an example of a quiz on karst formations. The answers follow:

1. Sinkholes, ridges, vertical shafts, disappearing streams, reappearing springs
2. Limestone, gypsum, dolostone
3. Acid rain that combines with carbon dioxide to form carbonic acid
4. The kras region in Slovenia; *karst* is a German word
5. Live a greener lifestyle—using biofuels more and fossil fuels less.

KEY POINTS

✘ Some students may take a long time finding an earthcache on the Internet. Make sure that they know how to access geocaching.com, how to make an inquiry when trying to find a cache (zip code, state, city, country), and how to recognize the earthcache symbol.

✘ Make students aware of the different geological features that they might be interested in and where those features might be found. This will help students in their online search for caches. For example, students might want to find a volcano (Hawaii or Washington), an escarpment (New York), a glacier (Alaska), limestone deposits (Wisconsin, Illinois, or Virginia), or even gems (North Carolina, New Mexico, Arizona, and many international sites).

VARIATIONS

✘ Take pictures of the geological features at an earthcache with a digital camera. Label the pictures and post them to share with others.

✘ Collect rock samples, fossils, and so on, from an earthcache. Identify the type of rock or fossil for each sample, and share the findings with other classes.

FIGURE 6.9

QUIZ ON KARST FORMATIONS

Name _____   Teacher _____

How much do you know about karst formations?

1. Name three or more identifying features of a karst formation.

2. Name an example of the soluble bedrock from which karsts are formed.

3. What is the cause of erosion that creates the features of the karsts?

4. Where did the term *karst formation* originate?

5. How can we help to reduce the amount of carbon emissions that create carbonic acid in the future?

From J.K. Taylor, D. Kremer, K. Pebworth, and P. Werner, 2010, *Geocaching for schools and communities* (Champaign, IL: Human Kinetics).

✖ Find an interesting geological feature where you live and create your own earthcache to share with others.

✖ Have the students decide where they might like to visit someday. That may be in the United States (Hawaii, Alaska, Colorado, California, New York) or even a foreign country (Germany, England, Afghanistan, India, China). Suggest that they try to find an earthcache in one of those places.

Social Studies 1

I Didn't Know That!

CONTENT AREA
History—local and state history

APPROPRIATE AGE GROUP
9- to 12-year-olds

OVERVIEW
Students will develop a list of questions about their school or community and will provide answers to those questions on a one-page description sheet. They will then create a geocache or waymark and register it online (including the one-page description and answer sheet) for others to visit.

OBJECTIVES
By participating in this learning experience, students will improve their ability to do the following:

✖ Develop knowledge of the history of their school and community.

✖ Cooperate with their classmates to create a registered site on geocaching.com or waymarking.com.

✖ Use the Internet and a GPS unit to discover information about historical events and places of significance in their area.

EQUIPMENT
A computer, a GPS unit, a container that is the appropriate size for the cache, trade items, a logbook, paper, and a pencil or pen

ORGANIZATION
This experience can be organized as a whole-class or small-group project.

DESCRIPTION
During this learning experience, the students will develop and register a geocache about the history of their school. They should follow all of the guidelines for creating a cache. (Go to geocaching.com and click on Hide & Seek a Cache. In the Hide a Cache area of the page, click the links to read the information for the cache listing requirements and guidelines and for how to hide a geocache.)

Step 1: Research the cache location. Where on the school grounds would be a good location for the cache? Consider a place away from car or pedestrian traffic and a place where the cache will not disturb ongoing classes or the environment. Some possibilities include near the flagpole, behind some shrubbery, or behind or under a loose rock by a wall. Be clever! Get permission from the school principal or board of education.

Step 2: Prepare your cache. Choose a container that will withstand the weather year-round, such as a clear, watertight plastic container or an ammunition box. Include a zippered plastic bag to further protect the contents of the cache. Label the cache as an "official geocache." Provide the name of the cache and appropriate contact information. (The contact is the teacher or class who will register as owners of the cache.)

Have the students investigate answers to questions about the history of their school; the students should create a sheet of information that will be found by visitors to this cache site (see figure 6.10). Register two or three specific questions for visitors to this cache to answer when logging the cache online. Have the students create a logbook that will be provided (along with a writing utensil) in the cache. Include a note to welcome the cache finder.

Lastly, have the students provide items for trading that will be put into the cache. Toys for children—such as action figures, key chains, games, and playing cards—are good items for trading. Other possibilities might include a few school pencils, decals, pins, or badges.

Step 3: Place your cache. You need to obtain accurate GPS coordinates for your geocache. Have three to five sets of students use a GPS unit and mark the waypoint coordinates. Then, average the readings to obtain your final waypoint marking. Once you have the waypoint, write it in permanent marker on the container and in the logbook. Put the logbook in a separate zippered plastic bag for extra protection, and place it in the cache container.

Step 4: Submit your cache. Have the students review the geocache listing guidelines again. Does your cache meet all the requirements for placement? If so, have the students fill out the online form, paying attention to the helpful notes provided. Make sure the description of your cache attracts geocachers to your location. Include descriptive attributes so that others can make a quick assessment of your cache. For example, specify whether the area is wheelchair accessible and whether the area is dog friendly. Have the children double-check the accuracy and the format of the cache information. Make any needed edits. After a review, the cache will be published for the general public.

Step 5: Maintain your cache. Once the cache is placed, the class is responsible for maintaining the cache and the area around it. Have the students return to the cache about once per week to make sure the cache is not affecting the area negatively and to check that the container is in good shape. Does the area look disturbed? Are visitors disrupting the landscape in any way? If concerns develop about the location, move the container and make appropriate changes to the online listing.

FIGURE 6.10

HISTORY OF OUR SCHOOL

Name _____   Teacher _____

How much do you know about your school?

1. What is the name of your school?

2. Why was this name chosen?

3. What year was the school built?

4. Who is the current principal of the school?

5. Who was the first principal of the school?

6. What is the school mascot?

7. What are the school colors?

8. What is the school enrollment?

9. What grade levels are enrolled in this school?

10. Who is the current teacher of the year in this school?

11. Who are some famous graduates of this school?

From J.K. Taylor, D. Kremer, K. Pebworth, and P. Werner, 2010, *Geocaching for schools and communities* (Champaign, IL: Human Kinetics).

After the cache is registered, have the students regularly check online to see who has logged the cache and provided answers to the history questions about the school. Develop a rotation schedule for different students to correspond with the cache visitors.

ASSESSMENT SUGGESTIONS

Develop a quiz to test the students' knowledge of the history of their own school or community (see figure 6.10). The quiz may be given orally or in writing.

KEY POINTS

✖ Make sure that everyone in the project has a contribution to make. Some can be in charge of gathering detailed information. Some can select the location to hide the cache and provide the latitude and longitude coordinates. Some can provide items to place in the cache. Some can enter data on the computer. Others can track people who visit the cache and communicate with them.

✖ Check all information for accuracy before entering data on the computer.

✖ Before registering the geocache, make sure that you get permission from the principal or board of education.

VARIATIONS

✖ Identify a local building of significance in your city. What year was it built? Who first occupied the building? Who occupies the building now? Has its use changed? Register the place in the buildings, history, or culture department of waymarking.com. Provide information about the history of this place. Have people who visit your new site provide answers to the questions you pose.

✖ Find a statue, memorial, monument, mural, or sculpture in your city. Register it in the appropriate department of waymarking.com. Have the people who visit your site register and take a digital picture of their visit or answer some questions about the location (i.e., about the statue, memorial, and so on). Ask the visitors to e-mail the picture or the answers to your class.

✖ Go online to waymarking.com and choose a historical department of interest, such as one related to art, music, buildings (perhaps the National Register of Historical Places), history, culture, memorials, or monuments. Find a place of interest close to your area. Using your GPS unit, visit the site and learn about this place of interest.

Social Studies 2

Where in the World?

CONTENT AREA

Geography—use of a map and compass

APPROPRIATE AGE GROUP

9- to 12-year-olds

OVERVIEW

Students will learn about map and compass terminology in a classroom setting. Then, they will go outside to complete several practical exercises by using a compass (or the compass on a GPS unit).

OBJECTIVES

By participating in this learning experience, students will improve their ability to do the following:

✖ Define common map and compass terms.

✖ Use a compass or GPS unit to determine direction of travel.

✖ Use a map and compass or GPS unit to find different locations around the school or at a park setting.

EQUIPMENT

A compass or GPS unit, a map of the school grounds, a 50- or 100-foot measuring tape, a protractor, a deck of playing cards or index cards for markers, paper, and a writing utensil

ORGANIZATION

Initial work will be whole-class instruction inside the classroom or outside on the playground or open-space area. Students will then work individually or in pairs to navigate a course using a compass or GPS unit.

DESCRIPTION

Begin instruction with a discussion about maps and compasses. Identify the parts of the compass and some common terminology—compass rose, housing, azimuth, base plate, direction-of-travel arrow, doghouse, cardinal points, bearing. For more advanced students, include other aspects such as aiming off, attack point, **declination, intercardinal points**, latitude, longitude, **magnetic north, grid north**, scale, **topographic map**, and so on. (Suggested references include www.thecompassstore.com; *Be an Expert With Map and Compass* by B. Kjellstrom [2009]; and *Wilderness Navigation: Finding Your Way Using Map, Compass, Altimeter, and GPS* by B. Burns and M. Burns [2004].)

While still inside the classroom, provide each student or pair of students with a compass or GPS unit. Teach them how to hold the compass or GPS unit properly and how to find and point in different directions (to do this with GPS units, you will need to be outside). Also, give each student a copy of a map of the school grounds. Teach students how to orient the map to the north and how to recognize different places around the school from the map (parking lot, playground, entrance, flagpole, and so on).

Go outside to an open area such as a grassy field. Have the students point in different directions using their compass or GPS unit. Orient them to where they are on the school map.

Spread the 50- or 100-foot measuring tape on the ground facing north to south or east to west. Have the students walk off a specific distance (50 feet) and count their steps. Have them do the same thing two or three more times and average their number of steps for that distance (e.g., 18 steps for 50 feet).

Give each student a playing card or index card. Have the students memorize their playing card or mark their index card with a special identifying symbol. Have the students spread out in scatter formation and place their card face-down at their feet. Choose one of the **cardinal points**—north (0 degrees), east (90 degrees), south (180 degrees), or west (270 degrees)—and have the students walk off 50 feet. Then, have them take a back bearing—for example, if they went north (0 degrees), they will return going south (180 degrees)—and walk back 50 feet to their point of origin (see figure 6.11). They will then turn over the card nearest their point of return and determine how close they come to arriving back at their card (i.e., how many steps away from their card). Choose another direction and back bearing and do this again. If students are comfortable with cardinal points, they may choose intercardinal points or any azimuth they want.

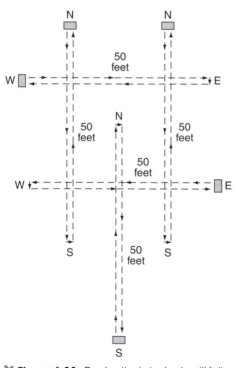

✖ Figure 6.11 Routes that students will follow in the Where in the World? activity.

Next, with the students still spread out and using their cards placed facedown at their feet, have the students walk off 50 feet in the direction of each of the cardinal points to make a square. Again, after completing this task, students will turn over the closest card to their feet and determine how close they come to their point of origin (i.e., how many steps away from their card). Then, have the students use intercardinal points or any azimuth to start, turn 90 degrees each time to make a square, and return to their point of origin. They should again check to see if they arrive at their cards.

Finally, have students repeat this exercise using a rectangle as the figure to walk. For example, the students walk north (0 degrees) for 50 feet, turn and walk east (90 degrees) for 100 feet, turn and walk south (180 degrees) for 50 feet, and turn and walk west (270 degrees) for 100 feet back to the point of origin. They then check to see if they arrive at their cards, determining how many steps away they are from their card. Next, have students use intercardinal points or any azimuth to start, turn 90 degrees each time, and again walk for 50, 100, 50, and 100 feet in sequence. When they return to the starting point, they again check to see how close they came to their cards.

ASSESSMENT SUGGESTIONS

Develop a scorecard for the compass activities similar to the one shown in figure 6.12. How close do students come to their card on their return to the point of origin? Start with 100 points and take away 2 points for each step they are from their cards.

Another way to assess this learning experience is to use a map of the school grounds and a compass or GPS unit. Identify specific places around the school and its grounds by labeling those places with a letter or number. Then, ask the students specific questions about what they find at each location or what degree bearing they would use to arrive at a location. Figure 6.13 shows a sample of what the map and questions could look like.

KEY POINTS

✖ Observe the students to make sure they take bearing readings properly. Their thumbs should be touching and their two index fingers should be touching and pointing in the intended direction (their fingers make a triangle with the index fingers pointing). Their body must also be squared with or facing the intended direction of travel.

✖ Have the students stride or march off a specific distance several times— 30, 50, or 100 feet. Make sure that their steps are regular or equidistant so that they are consistent in their distance traveled.

✖ Observe the students to make sure that they understand how to measure the angles and distances on a given square, rectangle, or triangle compass trial. If any students appear to be confused, pair them up with someone who is confident in their abilities.

VARIATIONS

✖ Have the students complete the compass activity using an equilateral triangle as a point of orientation (see figure 6.14). The students will need to take one bearing of their choice and walk a chosen distance. Then, they will add or subtract 120 degrees and walk the same distance. Finally, they will again add or subtract 120 degrees and walk the same distance. This will take them back to their point of origin. If students begin by taking a 30-degree bearing and walking 50 feet, they would then turn and take a bearing of 150 degrees for another 50 feet. Finally, they would turn and take a bearing of 270 degrees for 50 feet and return to their point of origin. Once students get the idea of how to measure the angles, they can begin by choosing any degree of bearing to start.

FIGURE 6.12

SCORECARD FOR COMPASS OR GPS EXPERIENCE

Name _____   Teacher _____

Cardinal Point and Back Bearing

North and south: Number of steps from home base _____ Score _____

East and west: Number of steps from home base_____ Score _____

Square

Trial 1: Number of steps from home base_____ Score _____

Trial 2: Number of steps from home base_____ Score _____

Rectangle

Trial 1: Number of steps from home base_____ Score _____

Trial 2: Number of steps from home base_____ Score _____

Total score _____

Average score _____

From J.K. Taylor, D. Kremer, K. Pebworth, and P. Werner, 2010, *Geocaching for schools and communities* (Champaign, IL: Human Kinetics).

FIGURE 6.13

ORIENTATION TO OUR SCHOOL

Name _____   Teacher _____

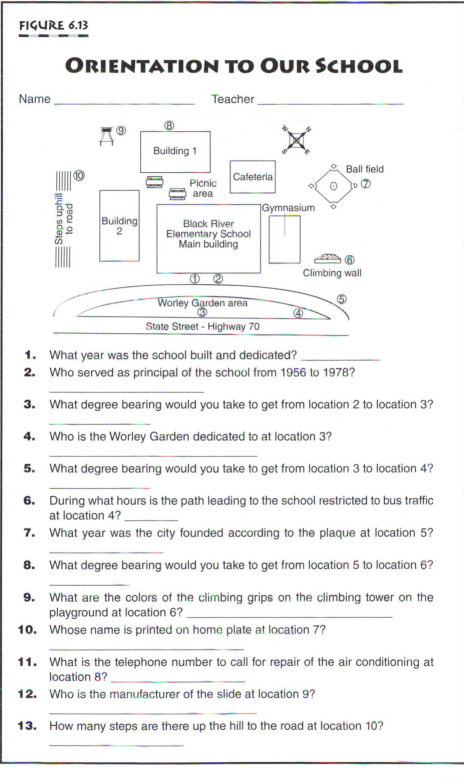

1. What year was the school built and dedicated? _____
2. Who served as principal of the school from 1956 to 1978?

    _____

3. What degree bearing would you take to get from location 2 to location 3?

    _____

4. Who is the Worley Garden dedicated to at location 3?

    _____

5. What degree bearing would you take to get from location 3 to location 4?

    _____

6. During what hours is the path leading to the school restricted to bus traffic at location 4? _____

7. What year was the city founded according to the plaque at location 5?

    _____

8. What degree bearing would you take to get from location 5 to location 6?

    _____

9. What are the colors of the climbing grips on the climbing tower on the playground at location 6? _____

10. Whose name is printed on home plate at location 7?

    _____

11. What is the telephone number to call for repair of the air conditioning at location 8? _____

12. Who is the manufacturer of the slide at location 9?

    _____

13. How many steps are there up the hill to the road at location 10?

    _____

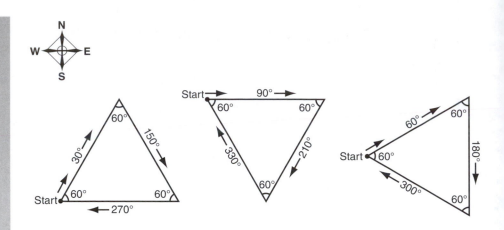

✖ Figure 6.14 Equilateral triangles.

✖ Have the students complete the compass activity using a 45-degree isosceles right triangle as a point of orientation (see figure 6.15). Using the formula of $a^2 + b^2 = c^2$, begin with horizontal and vertical sides of the triangle. If sides a and b are each 50 feet long, then the diagonal side is about 71 feet. If the students begin by taking a 0-degree bearing and walking for 50 feet, they would then turn, take a bearing of 135 degrees, and walk for 71 feet. Finally, they would turn, take a bearing of 270 degrees, and walk for 50 feet as they return to their point of origin. Or, they could start by walking 50 feet with a 270-degree bearing. They would then turn and take a 45-degree bearing for 71 feet. Finally, they would turn, take a bearing of 180 degrees, and walk for 50 feet back to their point of origin. They can begin by choosing any degree of bearing to start.

✖ Have the students complete the compass activity using a 3-4-5 right triangle (the angles measure 30, 60, and 90 degrees) as a point of orientation (see figure 6.16). Once again, begin by using the formula of $a^2 + b^2 = c^2$ and make the sides of the triangle horizontal and vertical. If side a equals 30 feet and side b equals 40 feet, then the diagonal side is 50 feet. If the students begin by taking a 0-degree bearing and walking for 40 feet, they would then turn, take a bearing of 150 degrees, and walk for 50 feet. Finally, they would turn and take a bearing of 270 degrees for 30 feet as they return to their point of origin. Or, they could start by walking 40 feet at a bearing of 0 degrees and then turn and take a 90-degree bearing for 30 feet. Then, they would turn, take a bearing of 210 degrees, and walk 50 feet back to their point of origin. Once students get the idea of how to measure the angles, they can begin by choosing any degree of bearing to start.

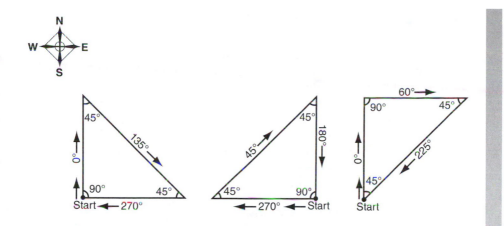

✖ **Figure 6.15** Isosceles triangles.

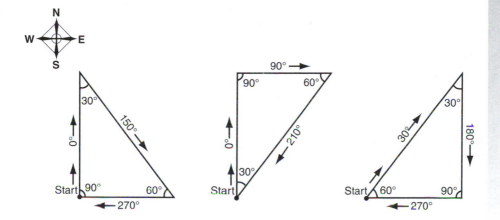

✖ **Figure 6.16** 30-60-90 right triangles.

Suggested Additional Learning Experiences

Following are suggestions for additional learning experiences. For each of these ideas, a name and a short description are provided to get you started in developing more lessons that integrate geocaching with disciplinary subjects. Take the ideas and run. Good luck!

Language Arts 1: Just Chatting

Encourage the students to go to the forums section of geocaching.com and ask questions or join a chat session regarding a topic of interest. Using technology such as GPS units and the Internet motivates students and provides them with opportunities to read, write, and speak to other cachers about their experiences. Groundspeak forums allow participants to receive a free online magazine for geocachers and benchmark hunters, read the latest announcements about geocaching, ask questions when getting started, discuss geocaching and related topics with others, share a great story about a cache hunt, and so on. Another good source for joining discussion groups is www.educaching.com.

Language Arts 2: Event Cache

Create and announce an event cache to be held at your school or a park and recreation site. Invite local cachers to attend. These geocachers can share their experiences through stories, and perhaps your students and their families will develop relationships with these cachers so they can go out caching together. Being with other cachers in a social situation allows students to develop better listening and speaking skills.

Mathematics 1: Point of Intersection

Find an intersection point of two lines based on four coordinates: A, B, C, and D (see figure 6.17). This experience can be carried out on the school playground, on a Frisbee golf course, or in a park or recreation area. After students find the coordinates for points A, B, C, and D, they need to draw lines from A to D and from B to C on graph paper using the numbers from the coordinate positions. They can then calculate the intersection of the two lines to find the coordinates for the final cache position (E).

Mathematics 2: The Law of Averages

Use the trip computer page on a GPS unit to teach students how to measure the total distance of their geocaching trip, their maximum speed traveled, their moving time, their time stopped, their average speed while moving, and their overall average speed.

Science 1: Sunrise, Sunset

Most GPS units have a sun and moon section on their main menu selection page. On the sun and moon page, you can also find the time of sunrise and sunset for a given day. Have students find the time of sunrise and sunset on a given day using the GPS unit. They should then project this out to the sunrise and sunset on a selected date (e.g., the Fourth of July, Christmas, New Year's Day, or their birthday).

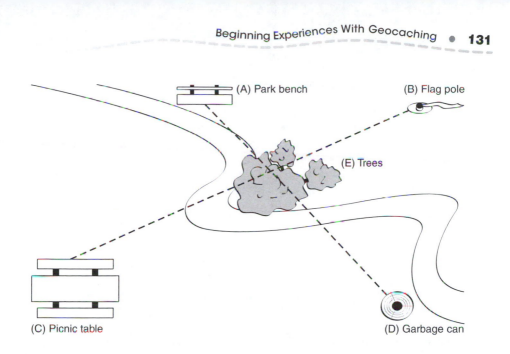

(A) Park bench

(B) Flag pole

(E) Trees

(C) Picnic table

(D) Garbage can

✖ **Figure 6.17** To find the final cache location, draw lines from points A to D and B to C and figure out where they intersect.

Science 2: Moon Up

Most GPS units have a sun and moon section on their main menu selection page. Have students find the days of the new moon, quarter moon, half moon, and full moon for a given month using a GPS. They should then project this out to different years.

Science 3: Benchmarks

Geologists and land surveyors have mapped the entire United States by placing survey markings in the ground. These markings are often placed in town squares and at the top of peaks. You probably walk by one every day. By confirming the continued location of these sites, geocachers are very helpful to the U.S. Geological Survey. Searching out these locations, documenting them by taking digital pictures, and posting the information and pictures will also allow others to learn where these sites are located. Some of these points haven't been visited and documented in a very long time, so you may be rediscovering long-neglected objects of American history as well.

Help students find a set of benchmarks in your local area and post confirmation of your findings to the U.S. Geological Society. Go to geocaching. com and click on Find a Benchmark. Then perform a search using your local zip code.

Science 4: How High Am I?

Help students determine the altitude of selected locations and the amount of ascent and descent on a specific trek using the GPS. Create a graph of the journey.

Social Studies 1 (Geography): How Many Ways Can I Get There?

When locating a geocache and deciding how to get there, teach the students how to use the various methods of tracking a site. On some types of GPS units, when you click Enter on the Go To option of the GPS unit of every geocache, you will be given a choice for how you will travel to get there— off road, fastest route, or shortest distance. Depending on whether they go to the cache in a family car, on a bicycle, or walking, they can choose the GPS function that is most appropriate for their method of travel.

Social Studies 2 (Geography): Rocking on the Road

Students can learn to use the rocker key (toggle button) on the GPS unit to find an intersection on a highway (interstate) or in a city that they might plan to visit or pass on a trip. For example, while on a trip, they might be traveling on an unfamiliar highway. With their GPS unit turned on to the map page, they can use the toggle button to move the location arrow from your present location ahead to an intersection or city where they may want to get gas, eat a meal, or stay overnight. On some types of GPS, they can enter that intersection or city and identify the gas stations, restaurants, hotels, and places of interest nearby. Provide students with multiple opportunities to practice this skill to ensure they have learned it thoroughly.

Social Studies 3 (Geography): Google Earth

Have the students go to http://earth.google.com. Have them register for Google Earth services (free). Then, have them type in a person's name (a friend or relative) and street address, including street name and number, city, state, and zip code. Then, simply click on Fly To that destination. Or, have them type in information for a place of interest (e.g., a downtown store, a park, or a swimming pool). Then, have them click on Fly To that location and zoom in to get an overhead view of it. Have them find out the latitude and longitude coordinates of the location and enter the coordinates on their GPS unit. Then, have them use the GPS unit to navigate to that location.

Social Studies 4 (Geography): Nowhere, Everywhere

A waymark is a physical location on the planet marked by coordinates (latitude and longitude) that are listed on the www.waymarking.com Web site. The Web site contains unique information for each waymark, and the waymarks are listed within various categories—cathedrals, steeples, cabooses, clocks, statues, and so on. The categories seem endless, and there are over 215,000 waymarks available.

Have the students go to waymarking.com. Have them find a location-less cache category of interest (e.g., abandoned train tunnels, sundials, fire trucks, glaciers, zoos, tree houses, British telephone booths). Have them enter the page for that cache and find out what information is provided. Perhaps they can go to a local place that is well known in a particular locationless cache category. Have the students take a picture with a digital camera of their visit to the site, and register online the date they visited the locationless cache.

Social Studies 5 (History): Did You Know?

Encourage students to learn interesting historical facts about every cache they visit. They might try to answer questions such as the following: Who was buried here? Who was the first mayor of the city? What year did an event (war battle, celebration, and so on) take place? Why was this park given its name? What year was the city founded? What year was this building built, or when did it burn down? Whom or what do the statues at this location represent?

Social Studies 6 (History): All Around Town

Many multicaches exist that conduct a tour of a local town or park and recreation area. Have students find one near where they live and complete the cache. Ask students what they learned about buildings of significance, sites with historical dates, and so on.

Social Studies 7 (History): Marking My Way

Have students locate various categories of interest on waymarking.com. For example, they may try searching for the following categories: statues of Lincoln or Washington, state historical markers, urban legends, veterans memorials, suspension bridges, gates of distinction, or national historical sites. Students should display the pages for the waymarks they find and should read them to learn about history.

chapter 7

ADVANCED EXPERIENCES WITH GEOCACHING

This chapter provides learning experiences with content that is appropriate for participants at the upper middle school and high school levels. These activities are ideal for participants who are 14 years of age and older. Many of these learning experiences involve physical activity. As mentioned previously, incorporating physical activity into traditionally sedentary subject areas is one of the benefits of geocaching. The learning experiences in this chapter demonstrate how—with creativity—you can integrate physical activity into any subject area. This gets participants more physically active and involves them in more hands-on learning. However, incorporating geocaching into these subject areas also means that you will need to create and place caches as well as program cache coordinates into GPS units. Alternatively, you may have the participants create and hide their own caches for a given learning experience. You can also teach the participants how to program coordinates into the GPS units and have them perform these steps as part of the learning experience.

Learning Experiences

This chapter provides two complete learning experiences for each of the four subject areas: language arts, mathematics, science, and social studies (see table 7.1). For each learning experience, the following information

Table 7.1

ADVANCED LEARNING EXPERIENCES WITH GEOCACHING

Discipline and skill concept	Name
LANGUAGE ARTS	
Locating print media in the library to facilitate the research process	Lost in the Library . . . NOT!
Reading, comprehension, and critical thinking to determine relevant information and the correct order of events	Which Came First . . . the Chicken or . . . ?
MATHEMATICS	
Solving logic problems using clues	Local Logics
Geometry, specifically triangles, the different types of triangles, and the language associated with triangles	Geodraw
SCIENCE	
Biological life science—phases of cell division	Cell Division—And We Aren't Talking Math!
Chemistry—chemical elements and element groups	It's ELEMENTary!
SOCIAL STUDIES	
History—westward expansion of the United States	Westward Ho!
Geography—state capitals and large cities in the United States	State of the Union

is provided: name, content area, overview, objectives, equipment, organization, complete description of the lesson, and assessment suggestions. In addition, key points on what to look for in participant responses and suggestions for modifying the learning experience are provided. Because all of the learning experiences are intended for participants ages 14 to 18, the age group is not specified for each one.

Remember, if GPS units are not available for these learning experiences, you can always develop directions to each hidden cache location using clues about the location, steps to take in a certain direction, or even compass directions to follow.

Finally, these learning experiences can be used in the classroom as well as in community and recreational settings. At the end of the chapter, suggested ideas for additional learning experiences are provided for each content area.

Language Arts 1

Lost in the Library . . . NOT!

CONTENT AREA
Locating print media in the library to facilitate the research process

OVERVIEW
Participants will explore the use of latitude and longitude coordinates in geocaching to identify specific cache sites; then participants will associate geocaching's use of latitude and longitude coordinates to identify specific cache sites with the library's use of call numbers to identify specific subject areas.

OBJECTIVES
By participating in this learning experience, participants will improve their ability to do the following:

- ✘ Understand the latitude and longitude coordinates used in geocaching to identify a specific location.
- ✘ Understand the classification system used by the local library.
- ✘ Identify subject areas and call numbers.
- ✘ Physically locate print materials in the library.

EQUIPMENT
GPS units (one per small group), enough cache containers to place a library classification subject category in each cache for each group, coordinates for specific cache sites in the area, subject categories for the classification system used by the local library, pencil and worksheet for each participant, and a map of the library (without call numbers indicated) for each participant

ORGANIZATION

This learning experience is a general introduction to the Dewey decimal classification system (using the second summary, hundreds division categories of that system). The learning experience alternates between a large- and small-group activity, beginning and ending as a large-group activity. When determining the number of categories to use, take into account the goal of the learning experience (i.e., overall introduction to the library or introduction to a specific area or subject area in the library), the size of the overall group, the number of GPS units available, and the number of caches you want to create and hide. For example, with a group of 30 participants and 10 GPS units, the participants could be divided into 10 groups of 3 per group. If you want to hide 6 caches, you would need 60 categories. Each cache would contain 10 categories, one category for each group to retrieve from each cache (see figure 7.1).

If you want to use fewer categories, the categories can be duplicated. After determining the categories and writing each category on a separate slip of paper, place enough categories in each cache so that each small group can collect one category per cache. Once the caches have been created, hide them and record the coordinates of their locations. Next, the coordinates for each hidden cache must be uploaded into the GPS units. Upload the coordinates yourself or teach the participants how to do this as part of the learning experience.

Libraries may use the Dewey decimal system or the Library of Congress classification system as a way to locate items in specific subject areas in the library. You can visit the Web site http://library.thinkquest.org/5002/ to review numerous resources that discuss the Dewey decimal classification system. The site includes group activities and quizzes for all levels of participants. Another good Web site is www.oclc.org/us/en/dewey/support/default.htm. For information about the Library of Congress classification system, you can visit www.loc.gov/catdir/cpso/lcco/.

DESCRIPTION

Begin this learning experience by holding a discussion with the entire group. Explain the use of GPS units and latitude and longitude coordinates as a way to pinpoint specific locations anywhere in the world. If a geocache is located close by, show the geocache and its coordinates to the group using the geocaching.com Web site. Then explain that a certain number of caches have been hidden in the area and that the participants' assignment is to use the GPS units to locate the caches and retrieve a category from each cache. Divide the participants into small groups and show them how to access the cache coordinates in the GPS unit. Send the participants out to locate the caches and retrieve the categories.

Once the caches have been found, reconvene the group and discuss how the right tools—in this case, the GPS unit and coordinates—enable a person to find a specific location rapidly. Then you can make the analogy to how libraries

FIGURE 7.1

Sixty Categories for the Dewey Decimal Classification, Second Summary, Hundreds Division

000	Computer science, knowledge & systems	420	English & Old English languages
030	Encyclopedias & books of facts	440	French & related languages
050	Magazines, journals & serials	460	Spanish & Portuguese languages
070	News media, journalism & publishing	470	Latin & Italic languages
080	Quotations	480	Classical & modern Greek languages
100	Philosophy	490	Other languages
150	Psychology	510	Mathematics
160	Logic	520	Astronomy
170	Ethics	530	Physics
180	Ancient, medieval & eastern philosophy	540	Chemistry
190	Modern western philosophy	550	Earth sciences & geology
220	The Bible	560	Fossils & prehistoric life
270	History of Christianity	570	Life sciences; biology
290	Other religions	580	Plants (Botany)
300	Social sciences, sociology & anthropology	590	Animals (Zoology)
320	Political science	610	Medicine & health
330	Economics	620	Engineering
370	Education	630	Agriculture
390	Customs, etiquette & folklore	660	Chemical engineering
410	Linguistics	690	Building & construction
		710	Landscaping & area planning
		720	Architecture
		730	Sculpture, ceramics & metalwork

(continued)

(continued)

750 Painting	870 Latin & Italic literatures
770 Photography & computer art	880 Classical & modern Greek literatures
780 Music	
790 Sports, games & entertainment	910 Geography & travel
	930 History of ancient world (to ca. 499)
810 American literature in English	940 History of Europe
820 English & Old English literatures	950 History of Asia
	960 History of Africa
850 Italian, Romanian & related literatures	970 History of North America
860 Spanish & Portuguese literatures	980 History of South America

organize their printed media to facilitate easy access of information. Explain the classification system used by the local library, referring to the categories the participants collected from the caches. See the Web site resources mentioned in the previous section for information about the two classification systems, or have the librarian speak about the classification system used by the local library. After this discussion, give the small groups a map of the library (minus call numbers) and challenge them to locate the categories in the library. Participants should mark the category sites on the library map provided to them. You may also require the participants to record a complete reference for a book found in that category as evidence of their work.

Once the participants have found their references, the group reconvenes and shares the discovered information so that each participant can compile a master map of the library resources. The participants can use this master map as a resource for future library visits and assignments.

ASSESSMENT SUGGESTIONS

✘ Have each participant complete and turn in a worksheet (figure 7.2); each group member records a different reference for each of the group's categories.

✘ Have participants turn in their individual library maps showing the category locations.

FIGURE 7.2

WORKSHEET FOR DEWEY DECIMAL CLASSIFICATION SYSTEM

Name _____ Teacher _____

First summary	Main classes	Second summary, hundred division	Resource example
000	General works		
100	Philosophy and psychology		
200	Religion		
300	Social sciences		
400	Language		
500	Natural science and mathematics		
600	Applied science and technology		
700	Fine arts and recreation		
800	Literature		
900	Geography and history		

From J.K. Taylor, D. Kremer, K. Pebworth, and P. Werner, 2010, *Geocaching for schools and communities* (Champaign, IL: Human Kinetics).

KEY POINTS

✗ Create a master map of cache locations and watch for small groups having difficulty in locating the caches. Assist them as needed.

✗ Link the use of latitude and longitude coordinates for finding specific geocaches to the use of library classification systems as an efficient way to locate specific materials in the library.

✗ Provide initial background information on the type of classification system used by the library where the participants will be completing the assignment.

✗ Provide participants with the schematic map of the library and check that each participant has completed a map at the end of the learning experience. Stress to the participants how useful this map will be for future library assignments.

VARIATIONS

✗ Place hints to each cache's location in sealed envelopes. Give these envelopes to the small groups for them to use if they need help finding the caches. The participants may gain additional points for returning the envelopes unopened at the end of the learning experience.

✗ Use the Dewey decimal third summary, thousands division classification if you want a learning experience targeted to a more specific topic, such as focusing on specific types of literature. Information on this classification can be found at www.oclc.org/us/en/dewey/support/default.htm.

✗ Discuss the correct way to write a reference for a paper. Have participants create a reference page using the appropriate referencing style (e.g., APA, MLA) from the resources gathered during the learning activity.

✗ Discuss the various types of resources that may be appropriate when writing a research paper, such as newspapers, encyclopedias, dictionaries, atlases, almanacs, books, and journals. Discuss which types of resources are preferable when writing a paper for different content areas such as English compared to science or history. Have participants locate those specific resources in the library and on their library map.

✗ Have participants repeat the learning experience at another library in the area—for example, the public library or a local college or university library.

Language Arts 2

Which Came First ... the Chicken or ... ?

CONTENT AREA

Reading, comprehension, and critical thinking to determine relevant information and the correct order of events

OVERVIEW

Participants will locate caches containing individual steps for two different recipes, determine which steps belong to each recipe, and organize the steps of each into the proper order. Comparisons can then be made to the importance of including relevant information in correct chronological order when summarizing a story or book.

OBJECTIVES

By participating in this learning experience, participants will improve their ability to do the following:

✖ Organize information in a logical order.

✖ Distinguish between relevant and nonrelevant information.

EQUIPMENT

GPS units (one per small group), enough cache containers to place one or two recipe steps in each container for each group, two recipes (each with multiple steps that have been divided into five to eight fragments to be hidden in the caches), and pencils

ORGANIZATION

This learning experience alternates between large- and small-group activity, beginning and ending as a large-group activity. The size of the small groups depends on the number of available GPS units. Before the learning experience, separate the recipes into steps (see figure 7.3). Each cache will contain multiple copies of one step from each of the two recipes (do not include the names of the recipes). The number of copies in each cache is determined by the number of small groups.

Once the caches have been created, hide them and record the coordinates of their locations. The coordinates for each hidden cache must then be uploaded into the GPS units. Upload the coordinates into the GPS units yourself or teach the participants how to do this as part of the learning experience.

DESCRIPTION

Begin this learning experience by holding a discussion with the entire group. Discuss the importance of relevance and order when communicating. Relevance involves including information that relates directly to the topic and leaving out information that is not related to what is being communicated. Order involves putting events into a chronological time frame in which they need to or should occur. Examples of order include providing the correct order of roads to follow and turns to make when giving someone directions to your house, following the correct order of steps when cooking, and relaying the correct order of events when telling a story.

Next, explain the use of GPS units and latitude and longitude coordinates as a way to pinpoint specific locations anywhere in the world. If a geocache is located close by, show the geocache and its coordinates to the group using

FIGURE 7.3

RECIPE STEPS

Recipe: apple pie	Recipe: fruitcake
Ingredients: apples, cinnamon, flour, lemon juice, lemon peel, margarine, nutmeg, pie pastry, sugar	Ingredients: baking powder, butter, eggs, extract, flour, fruit, jelly, nuts, orange juice, sugar, salt
Roll out half of the pastry and line a 9-inch pie plate.	Preheat the oven to 300° F. In a large bowl, combine the fruits and nuts. Toss with flour until the fruits and nuts are well coated.
In a small bowl, create a sugar mixture by combining sugar, flour, cinnamon, nutmeg, lemon peel, and lemon juice.	In another large bowl, beat the butter with sugar until light and fluffy using a mixer at medium speed.
Place half of the thinly sliced apples in the piecrust. Sprinkle with half of the sugar mixture. Top with the rest of the apples, then the remaining sugar mixture.	To the butter and sugar mixture, add flour, baking powder, salt, eggs, extract, and orange juice, beating at low speed until well mixed.
Dot the apple filling with margarine. Preheat the oven to 425° F.	Increase the speed of the mixer to medium and beat the batter 4 minutes longer.
Roll out the remaining pastry for the top crust. Place the crust over the apple filling.	With a spoon, stir the fruit and nut mixture into the batter until well mixed.
Fold the overhang of the top-crust pastry under then bring it up over the rim of the pie plate. Pinch to form a high edge.	Spoon the batter evenly into a pan and then bake for 3 hours.
Bake the pie for 40 to 50 minutes or until the crust is golden.	Before serving, melt jelly over low heat to form a glaze, brush it on the cake, and let the glaze set.

From J.K. Taylor, D. Kremer, K. Pebworth, and P. Werner, 2010, *Geocaching for schools and communities* (Champaign, IL: Human Kinetics).

the geocaching.com Web site. Then explain that a certain number of caches have been hidden in the area that contain steps to two different recipes. Tell the participants that their assignment is to use the GPS units to locate the caches and retrieve the recipe steps from each cache.

Divide the participants into small groups and show them how to access the cache coordinates in the GPS unit. Send the participants out to locate the caches and retrieve the recipe steps. Once the participants have found all the caches and retrieved the recipe steps, they should read through the steps. As they do this, the participants should use key words and phrases to determine which steps belong to each of the two recipes and the correct order of those steps. Groups can then guess what the recipe makes.

After each group has completed the task, bring everyone together again to assess whether the recipe steps were correctly separated and placed in the correct order. See if the groups correctly identified what the recipe makes. Then conduct a discussion of what happens to the product if the recipe steps are not placed in the correct order or if steps from the wrong recipe are included. This can lead to a discussion about the importance of relevance and correct chronological order when summarizing a story or book. More specifically, the discussion can revolve around how inclusion of relevant information in the correct chronological order adds to the reader's understanding, while irrelevant information or information that is out of order may confuse the reader.

ASSESSMENT SUGGESTIONS

✖ Have participants highlight key words in the recipe steps that help them identify steps that belong to the same recipe. For example, ingredients in the individual steps can be compared to the ingredient list to determine if they match up or not.

✖ Have participants circle key words and phrases that help determine the correct sequence of steps for each recipe. For example, with the apple pie recipe, the pastry has to be placed in the pie plate before the apples can be placed in the pie crust, and the oven has to be preheated before the pie can be baked. For the fruitcake recipe, the butter and sugar mixture needs to be created before the flour (and other ingredients) can be added to it, and the mixture has to be mixed at a low speed before the mixer speed can be increased to medium speed.

✖ Have participants turn in their work before the group discussion.

KEY POINTS

✖ Create a master map of the cache locations and watch for small groups having difficulty in locating the caches. Assist them as needed.

✖ Link the concepts of relevance and order in recipes to relevance and order when summarizing stories or books.

✖ If necessary, assist participants in locating key words that distinguish one recipe from the other.

✖ If necessary, assist participants in locating key terms or phrases that are indicative of chronological order.

VARIATIONS

✖ Place hints to each cache's location in sealed envelopes. Give these envelopes to the small groups for them to use if they need help finding the caches. Participants may gain additional points for returning the envelopes unopened at the end of the learning experience.

✖ Have the ingredients available so the participants can try out their assembled recipe steps to see if they made the correct decisions.

✖ After the group has read a story or book, choose several key events from the story, hide copies of those events in caches, and have the participants repeat the assignment with the story events.

✖ After the group has read a story or book, place copies of two key events in a cache. Have participants search for the caches and determine which event occurred first for each pair of key events.

✖ After the group has read a story or book, place copies of one key event and one irrelevant event in a cache. Have participants search for the caches and determine which event is key and which event is irrelevant.

✖ Have participants create their own chronological story and hide the segments in caches. Other participants in the class must then find the caches and put the story segments in the correct order.

✖ Leave out the end of a short story from the hidden caches and have participants write their own logical, creative ending.

✖ Leave out a key segment of the story from the hidden caches and see if the participants can determine the missing segment. Another option is to let the participants write their own segment to fill in the missing information.

Mathematics 1

Local Logics

CONTENT AREA
Solving logic problems using clues

OVERVIEW
Participants will locate caches that contain clues to a logic problem. After locating all the clues, participants will use the clues to solve the logic problem.

OBJECTIVES
By participating in this learning experience, participants will improve their ability to do the following:

✖ Think in a logical and organized fashion.
✖ Use facts and logic to help solve a problem.
✖ Use the process of elimination to help solve a problem.

EQUIPMENT

GPS units (one per small group), enough cache containers so that each clue to the logic problem can be placed in a separate cache, one copy of the logic problem grid for each participant, logic problem clues to be hidden in the caches, and pencils

ORGANIZATION

This learning experience alternates between large- and small-group activity, beginning and ending as a large-group activity. The size of the small groups depends on the number of available GPS units. Before the learning experience, separate the logic problem into its individual clues and create a grid for use when solving the logic problem (figure 7.4).

Each cache will contain multiple copies of a single clue from the logic problem. The number of copies in each cache is determined by the number of small groups. Once the caches have been created, hide the caches and record the coordinates of their locations. The coordinates for each hidden cache must then be uploaded into the GPS units. Upload the coordinates yourself or teach the participants how to do this as part of the learning experience.

DESCRIPTION

With the whole group, discuss how to solve logic problems, including the use of the grid. Using the logic problem from figure 7.5 (Who Wore the Shirt?), demonstrate how a clue provides information about a person identified in the clue. For example, if a clue states that Tameka wore the blue shirt, we know that she did not wear any other color shirt. Thus, we can put a check mark in the Blue column for Tameka and we can mark an X in the Yellow, Red, and Green columns for Tameka.

Explain that clues also provide information about people who are not identified in the clue. For example, from the clue that Tameka wore the blue shirt, we now know that Kanesha, Bob, and Henry did not wear the blue shirt. Thus, in the Blue column, we can mark an X for Kanesha, Bob, and Henry.

From the next clue, we know that Bob and Henry wear shirt colors that share letters with the letters in their name, so several possible shirt colors can be linked to them.

✖ Bob's possible colors are blue and yellow. However, because we know that Tameka wore the blue shirt, that means Bob wore the yellow shirt. In Bob's row, we can check Yellow and X the other color options.

✖ Henry's possible colors are blue, yellow, red, and green. However, we know that Tameka wore the blue shirt and Bob wore the yellow shirt. That narrows Henry's shirt color to red or green.

From the final clue, which states that the boys did not wear the green shirt, we can determine that Henry wore the red shirt. In Henry's row, we can check Red and X the other color options.

Finally, by process of elimination, we can determine that Kanesha wore the green shirt. In Kanesha's row, we can check Green and X the other shirt colors (see figure 7.6).

FIGURE 7.4

SIMPLE LOGIC PROBLEM: WHO'S GOT THE MOST?

Name _____ Teacher _____

Four people are discussing who has the most contacts on their cell phone. See if you can figure it out.

1. Lisa has more phone contacts than Maleek.

2. Vanessa has fewer phone contacts than Jerome.

3. Vanessa has 20 more phone contacts than Maleek.

4. Jerome has more phone contacts than Lisa.

	40 contacts	50 contacts	60 contacts	70 contacts
Lisa				
Maleek				
Jerome				
Vanessa				

From J.K. Taylor, D. Kremer, K. Pebworth, and P. Werner, 2010, *Geocaching for schools and communities* (Champaign, IL: Human Kinetics).

FIGURE 7.5

WHO WORE THE SHIRT?

Name _____ Teacher _____

1. Tameka wore the blue shirt.

2. Bob and Henry wore shirt colors that share letters with the letters in their name.

3. The boys did not wear the green shirt.

	Blue	Yellow	Red	Green
Tameka				
Kanesha				
Bob				
Henry				

FIGURE 7.6

SOLUTION TO WHO WORE THE SHIRT?

	Blue	Yellow	Red	Green
Tameka	✓	X	X	X
Kanesha	X	X	X	✓
Bob	X	✓	X	X
Henry	X	X	✓	X

Next, tell the participants that they are going to solve a new logic problem, and give them a copy of the grid for solving the simple logic problem: Who's Got the Most? (figure 7.4).

Explain the use of GPS units and latitude and longitude coordinates as a way to pinpoint specific locations anywhere in the world. If a geocache is located close by, show the geocache and its coordinates to the group using the geocaching.com Web site. Then explain that a certain number of caches have been hidden in the area. Tell the participants that their assignment is to use the GPS units to locate the caches and retrieve one logic problem clue from each hidden cache. Divide the participants into small groups and show them how to access the cache coordinates in the GPS unit. Send the participants out to locate the caches and retrieve the clues. Once the participants have found the caches and retrieved the clues, they read through the clues and use the grid to solve the logic problem. After each group has completed the task, the group reconvenes as a whole to discuss how each clue provided information to help solve the problem.

ASSESSMENT SUGGESTIONS

At the end of the learning experience, collect each participant's completed grid and answer to the logic problem. Check these for completeness and accuracy.

KEY POINTS

✘ Create a master map of the cache locations and watch for small groups having difficulty in locating the caches. Assist them as needed.

✘ Look for participants who are having difficulty using the grid. Remind them that a clue not only tells what is true but also rules out what cannot be true, which needs to be marked on the grid as well.

✘ Remind participants that the process of elimination also provides answers to the logic problem.

✘ Answers to the problem in figure 7.4 are as follows: Lisa has 50 contacts, Maleek has 40 contacts, Jerome has 70 contacts, and Vanessa has 60 contacts.

VARIATIONS

✘ Place hints to each cache's location in sealed envelopes. Give these envelopes to the small groups for them to use if they need help finding the caches. Participants may gain additional points for returning the envelopes unopened at the end of the learning experience.

✘ Start with a simple logic problem, such as the one in figure 7.4, and progress to more complex logic problems, such as the one in figure 7.7. (Answers for figure 7.7: Jerry Johnson's favorite sport is basketball; Marcus Masters' favorite sport is baseball; Kenya Masters' favorite sport is soccer; and Samuel Smith's favorite sport is football.)

✘ Send each group out to find and retrieve a single clue from a single cache. Then the entire group can work together to solve the logic problem, discussing what is learned from each clue as the clues are read aloud.

✘ Send each group out to find and retrieve a single logic problem from a single cache. Each group tries to solve their problem individually or as a group as quickly as possible.

✘ Have the participants create their own logic problems to be used in this learning experience.

Mathematics 2

Geodraw

CONTENT AREA

Geometry, specifically triangles, the different types of triangles, and the language associated with triangles

OVERVIEW

Participants will investigate the different types of triangles, the language of triangles, and how the various types of triangles differ from one another in side lengths and angles.

OBJECTIVES

By participating in this learning experience, participants will improve their ability to do the following:

✘ Demonstrate the shapes associated with different types of triangles.

✘ Correctly identify different types of triangles by their side lengths and angles.

FIGURE 7.7

COMPLEX LOGIC PROBLEM: FAVORITE SPORTS

Name _____ Teacher _____

Four friends were discussing their favorite sports. Their favorite sports were baseball, football, basketball, and soccer. From the statements that follow, determine the last name of each friend as well as each friend's favorite sport.

1. Marcus and Kenya, neither of whom like football or basketball, are brother and sister.
2. The Smith boy lives across the street from Marcus and Kenya. He doesn't like basketball.
3. Jerry lives several blocks away, and he doesn't like football.
4. The boy who likes baseball is not Samuel.
5. One of the Masters likes soccer.

	Baseball	Football	Basketball	Soccer		Johnson	Smith	Masters
Jerry								
Marcus								
Kenya								
Samuel								
Johnson								
Smith								
Masters								

From J.K. Taylor, D. Kremer, K. Pebworth, and P. Werner, 2010, *Geocaching for schools and communities* (Champaign, IL: Human Kinetics).

✖ Draw different types of triangles to scale on graph paper.

✖ Use correct language associated with triangles.

EQUIPMENT

Three small cones per group, GPS units (one per small group), pencils, paper, and graph paper for each participant (graph paper can be printed for free from numerous Internet sources such as www.printfreegraphpaper.com)

ORGANIZATION

This learning experience alternates between large- and small-group activity, beginning and ending as a large-group activity. Before the learning experience, write the names of the different types of triangles (right, equilateral, isosceles, scalene, acute, obtuse) on slips of paper and fold them.

DESCRIPTION

With the whole group, discuss the components of a triangle (three sides and three angles that add up to 180 degrees). Then introduce the different types of triangles (right, equilateral, isosceles, scalene, acute, and obtuse). Visit www.mathwarehouse.com for information about types of triangles, or refer to figure 7.8.

Participants can draw the triangles on graph paper and identify key points for each type of triangle. Next, divide the participants into groups of four and show them how to read and write the latitude and longitude coordinates shown on the GPS unit. Each small group comes up with a group name and then chooses a slip of paper that has a type of triangle written on it. With a GPS unit, the triangle information, and three cones in hand, each small group moves to an open outside area.

The first assignment for the small groups is to re-create their triangle, marking the three corners of the triangle using cones and recording the coordinates of each corner using the GPS. Three of the participants move to positions that create their specific triangle. The fourth participant is responsible for making sure the triangle shape is correct. Once the correct triangle shape is made, the fourth participant travels to each triangle corner with the GPS and writes down the latitude and longitude coordinates on a piece of paper that has the small group's name on it. The cones are left on the ground to mark the triangle.

When each small group has created their triangle and written down the coordinates, groups exchange triangle coordinates with other groups. Small groups, using their GPS and the new triangle coordinates, then identify the cones that correspond to their new triangle coordinates. As the new triangles are identified, the small groups draw the appropriate triangle on their graph paper to scale and label the triangle by its name and by the name of the small group that created it. Individual groups continue to exchange coordinates until they have correctly identified, drawn to scale, and labeled all the triangles created. The group then reconvenes as a whole, and each small group checks the other small groups' drawings to see if their triangle was correctly drawn. You can confirm the accuracy of the drawings and conduct a question-and-answer session with the group to reinforce and check for understanding regarding the types of triangles.

FIGURE 7.8

TYPES OF TRIANGLES

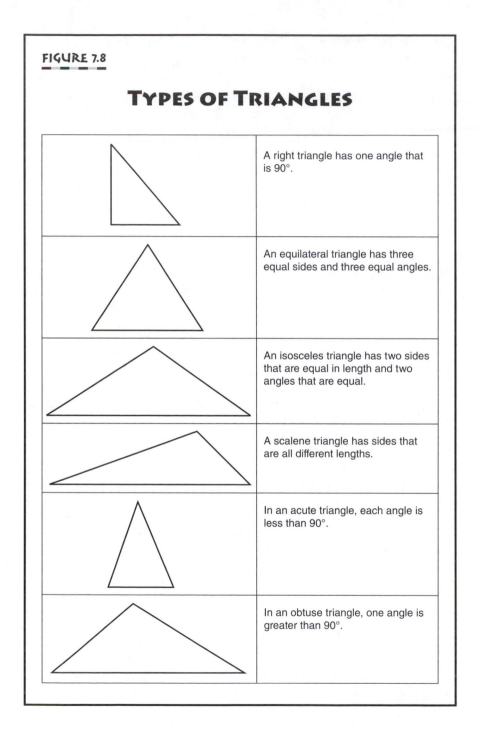

	A right triangle has one angle that is 90°.
	An equilateral triangle has three equal sides and three equal angles.
	An isosceles triangle has two sides that are equal in length and two angles that are equal.
	A scalene triangle has sides that are all different lengths.
	In an acute triangle, each angle is less than 90°.
	In an obtuse triangle, one angle is greater than 90°.

ASSESSMENT SUGGESTIONS

✘ Before moving the learning experience outside, list the names of the triangles on the board and have each participant draw each type of triangle and correctly label it on graph paper. Check each participant's drawings for accuracy.

✘ Once the learning experience has moved outside, check each group's triangle shape for accuracy before the group records the coordinates using the GPS.

✘ Have each group turn in their labeled triangle drawings so you can check them for accuracy.

✘ Remind participants to draw the triangles to scale to ensure they utilize some type of process to measure the three sides of each triangle.

KEY POINTS

✘ Define specific areas for each group to work in. This will prevent groups from overlapping and will help keep triangle sizes appropriate (not too small, not too large).

✘ Discuss ways to create sides of equal and unequal length. If two sides of the triangle are supposed to be equal, the number of steps for each side should be equal. Likewise, if two sides are supposed to be unequal, the number of steps for each side should be different. The participant who is responsible for recording the corner coordinates (i.e., the fourth participant in the group) should count the number of steps between triangle corners and make sure the side lengths are appropriate (equal or unequal) for the group's triangle.

✘ To help the groups keep track of which triangles they have correctly re-created and identified, have each group create a group name and write their group name on the sheet of paper containing their triangle's coordinates. When groups exchange coordinates and correctly identify a triangle by its coordinates, they should write their group name on the coordinate sheet for that triangle, indicating that they have solved that triangle. This will enable the groups to easily determine which triangles they have solved and which ones they still need to solve.

✘ To keep groups on task, give them a specific amount of time (e.g., 10 minutes) to create their triangles.

VARIATIONS

✘ Have the small groups remove the cones marking the corners of their triangles. Groups then have to rely solely on the GPS to complete the learning experience.

✘ Have small groups create triangles that overlap other groups' triangles. Groups then have to rely on the GPS to correctly identify the cones associated with individual triangles as they complete the learning experience.

✘ After the small groups have determined the triangles created by other groups and drawn those triangles on graph paper, have them use protractors to measure the angles of those triangles. Small groups can then compare results to see who drew the triangles and measured the angles correctly.

Science 1

Cell Division—And We Aren't Talking Math!

CONTENT AREA
Biological life science—phases of cell division

OVERVIEW
This self-test learning experience occurs at the conclusion of a unit covering mitosis, allowing participants to assess their knowledge of the phases of mitosis and the activity that occurs in each phase.

OBJECTIVES
By participating in this learning experience, participants will improve their ability to do the following:

✖ Identify the phases of mitosis.

✖ Identify the activity that occurs in each phase of mitosis.

EQUIPMENT
GPS units (one per small group), enough cache containers to place one unlabeled picture of a phase of mitosis (interphase, prophase, metaphase, anaphase, telophase, and cytokinesis) in each cache for each student, pictures depicting the phases of mitosis (try looking for these at http://library.thinkquest. org/20465/mitosis.html), pencils, and paper

ORGANIZATION
This learning experience alternates between large- and small-group activity, beginning and ending as a large-group activity. The size of the small groups depends on the number of available GPS units. Before the learning experience, make copies of pictures of mitosis and separate them into individual pictures. Each cache will contain multiple copies of one step of mitosis, one copy for each participant. Once the caches have been created, hide the caches and record the coordinates of their locations. The coordinates for each hidden cache must then be uploaded into the GPS units. Upload the coordinates yourself or teach the participants how to do this as part of the learning experience.

DESCRIPTION
After teaching a unit on mitosis, conduct a whole-group discussion to review the phases of mitosis and what happens within each phase. Answer any questions from the participants. Next, explain the use of GPS units and latitude and longitude coordinates as a way to pinpoint specific locations anywhere in the world. If a geocache is located close by, show the geocache and its coordinates to the group using the geocaching.com Web site. Then explain that a certain number of caches have been hidden in the area. Tell the participants that their assignment is to use the GPS units to locate the caches and retrieve the phases of mitosis from each cache. Each participant should retrieve one phase of mitosis from each cache.

Divide the participants into small groups and show them how to access the cache coordinates in the GPS unit. Send the participants out to locate the caches and retrieve the phases of mitosis. Once the caches have been found and each participant has a copy of all the phases of mitosis, participants place the pictures in the correct order. Participants then write down the name of each phase and record what happens in each phase.

ASSESSMENT SUGGESTIONS

✘ Have participants turn in their completed work for grading.

✘ Check the participants' work for the correct order of phases before they label and describe the phases.

✘ Use a worksheet that contains descriptions of the phases, and have the participants name the phases and match the pictures to the correct phase names. Check their work for accuracy.

KEY POINTS

✘ Create a master map of the cache locations and watch for small groups having difficulty in locating the caches. Assist them as needed.

✘ Have the participants review the phases of mitosis and what occurs in each phase before they go searching for the caches.

✘ Teach participants some techniques to help them remember the phases of mitosis. For example, in the metaphase, the chromosomes meet in the middle; to remember this, participants can relate *meta* to *meet.* During the anaphase, chromosome pairs separate or come apart and move to their respective poles. Participants can remember this by keeping in mind that, in anatomical terms, *ana-* means to cut apart.

VARIATIONS

✘ Place hints to each cache's location in sealed envelopes. Give these envelopes to the small groups for them to use if they need help finding the caches. Participants may gain additional points for returning the envelopes unopened at the end of the learning experience.

✘ Have participants draw the phases of mitosis and use those pictures when creating the caches.

✘ Create caches, with each cache containing a picture of a phase, a phase name, and a description of a phase. Participants collect the three items from each of the caches and after finding all caches and collecting all items, match the appropriate items together for each phase.

✘ Conduct the learning experience using other science concepts that can be divided into a name and a description. For example, for the human body, the systems of the body and their functions can be hidden in numerous caches for the participants to find and match together correctly. Another variation would be to hide the functions of each system in caches and have the participants correctly identify each system by its function.

Science 2

It's ELEMENTary!

CONTENT AREA

Chemistry—chemical elements and element groups

OVERVIEW

As part of a unit on the periodic table, participants will identify elements by their chemical symbol and determine the element group that the elements belong to.

OBJECTIVES

By participating in this learning experience, participants will improve their ability to do the following:

✖ Identify chemical elements in each of the element groups.

✖ Identify chemical elements by their symbol.

✖ Identify the location of element groups on the periodic table.

EQUIPMENT

GPS units (one per small group), nine geocache containers, chemical symbols for several elements in each of the nine element groups (enough copies for each participant to have one copy of each), pencils, and the periodic table (enough copies for each participant to have one copy; see figure 7.9)

ORGANIZATION

This learning experience alternates between large- and small-group activity, beginning and ending as a large-group activity. The size of the small groups depends on the number of available GPS units. Before the learning experience, identify the symbols for chemical elements as well as the element groups they belong to. Each cache will contain multiple copies of several chemical symbols from a single unnamed element group. The number of copies in each cache is determined by the number of participants involved in the learning experience.

Once the caches have been created, hide the caches and record the coordinates of their locations. The coordinates for each hidden cache must then be uploaded into the GPS units. Upload the coordinates yourself or teach the participants how to do this as part of the learning experience.

DESCRIPTION

As part of a unit on the periodic table, discuss how the elements are divided into nine groups based on their properties (alkali metals, other metals, halogens, alkaline earth metals, metalloids, noble gases, transitional metals, nonmetals, and rare earth elements). Identify the chemical symbols for elements in each group that the participants are expected to know. Next, still with the entire group of participants, explain the use of GPS units and latitude and longitude coordinates as a way to pinpoint specific locations anywhere in the world. If a geocache is located close

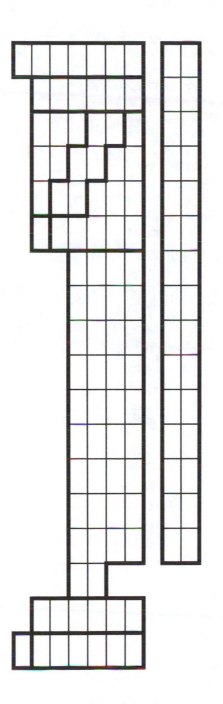

✕ Figure 7.9 A blank periodic table, separated by element group.

From J.K. Taylor, D. Kremer, K. Pebworth, and P. Werner, 2010, *Geocaching for schools and communities* (Champaign, IL: Human Kinetics).

by, show the geocache and its coordinates to the group using the geocaching. com Web site. Then explain that nine caches—one for each element group—have been hidden in the area. Tell the participants that their assignment is to use the GPS units to locate the caches and retrieve copies of the chemical elements from each cache (one copy of each element for each participant in the group).

Divide the participants into small groups and show them how to access the cache coordinates in the GPS unit. Send the participants out to locate the caches and retrieve the chemical symbols. Once the participants have found the caches and retrieved the chemical symbols, they can continue working in groups or work independently. The participants must identify the elements associated with the symbols and then identify what element group those elements belong to. It may be helpful to provide the participants with a blank copy of the periodic table (see figure 7.9).

Examples of element groups, chemical symbols, and element names:

Alkali metals
Li (lithium)
Na (sodium)
K (potassium)

Other metals
Al (aluminum)
Sn (tin)
Pb (lead)

Halogens
Cl (chlorine)
Br (bromine)
I (iodine)

Alkaline earth metals
Mg (magnesium)
Ca (calcium)
Ba (barium)

Metalloids
B (boron)
Si (silicon)
As (arsenic)

Noble gases
He (helium)
Ne (neon)
Kr (krypton)

Transitional metals
Ti (titanium)
Fe (iron)
Cu (copper)
Zn (zinc)
Ag (silver)
Au (gold)

Nonmetals
H (hydrogen)
C (carbon)
N (nitrogen)
O (oxygen)
P (phosphorus)

Rare earth elements
Ce (cerium)
Eu (europium)
Yb (ytterbium)
U (uranium)
Pu (plutonium)
Am (americium)

ASSESSMENT SUGGESTIONS

✗ Have the groups compete to see which group can correctly identify the most elements before allowing the participants to use their textbooks to complete the assignment.

✗ After the learning experience is complete and the group has reviewed the answers, give the participants a quiz that requires them to identify elements by their symbols and by their element group.

KEY POINTS

✘ Create a master map of the cache locations and watch for small groups having difficulty in locating the caches. Assist them as needed.

✘ Match weak and strong participants together in small groups to assist each other in identifying the correct elements and element groups.

VARIATIONS

✘ Place hints to each cache's location in sealed envelopes. Give these envelopes to the small groups for them to use if they need help finding the caches. Participants may gain additional points for returning the envelopes unopened at the end of the learning experience.

✘ As a culminating study session for the unit, place all the chemical symbols that the participants are required to know in the caches by element group; the number of elements that each group should collect from each cache will be stated in the cache. After identifying each element and element group, the small groups can compete to place their symbols in the correct locations on a blank periodic table. Ensure that all participants are involved by requiring each one to place a certain number of elements on the periodic table (this number will depend on class size and the number of elements in the caches).

✘ Using figure 7.9, separate the periodic table into element groups by cutting along the dark lines. Place enough copies of each cutout section in separate caches for each participant or small group to locate and collect. After collecting each section, the participant's or small group's assignment is to place each cutout section in the correct location on an outline of the periodic table (figure 7.10) and to correctly identify the element group that each section represents.

Social Studies 1

Westward Ho!

CONTENT AREA

History—westward expansion of the United States

OVERVIEW

This learning experience introduces basic facts about the westward expansion before an in-depth study of the topic.

OBJECTIVES

By participating in this learning experience, participants will improve their ability to do the following:

✘ Identify the land deals in U.S. history that created the land mass known as the United States.

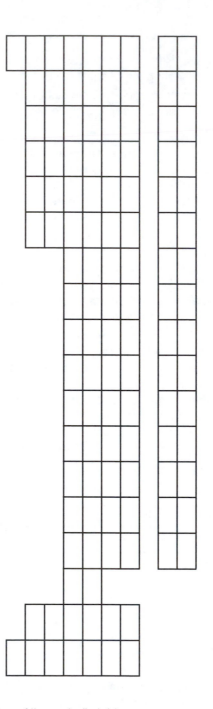

✖ Figure 7.10 Outline of the periodic table.

From J.K. Taylor, D. Kremer, K. Pebworth, and P. Werner, 2010, *Geocaching for schools and communities* (Champaign, IL: Human Kinetics).

✖ Identify countries that the United States acquired land from through wars, treaties, and purchases—and identify when the land was acquired.

✖ Identify the U.S. presidents in office during the land deals that created the United States.

EQUIPMENT

GPS units (one per small group), eight cache containers (information about one land deal will be placed in each cache), and facts associated with the westward expansion

ORGANIZATION

This learning experience alternates between large- and small-group activity, beginning and ending as a large-group activity. The size of the small groups depends on the number of available GPS units. Before the learning experience, compile pertinent facts about the westward expansion (see figure 7.11).

Each cache will contain pertinent facts about one territory acquired by the United States during the westward expansion. Once the caches have been created, hide the caches and record the coordinates of their locations. The coordinates for each hidden cache must then be uploaded into the GPS units. Upload the coordinates yourself or teach the participants how to do this as part of the learning experience.

DESCRIPTION

With the entire group together, explain the use of GPS units and latitude and longitude coordinates as a way to pinpoint specific locations anywhere in the world. If a geocache is located close by, show the geocache and its coordinates to the group using the geocaching.com Web site. Then explain that eight caches have been hidden in the area and that those caches contain facts about land deals during the westward expansion of the United States. Tell the participants that their assignment is to use the GPS units to locate the caches and then read the facts about each land deal. The goal is for each small group to remember as many facts as possible about the various land deals they will be reading about. Let the participants know that they will be quizzed on what they remember.

Divide the participants into small groups and show them how to access the cache coordinates in the GPS unit. Send the participants out to locate the caches and read the fact sheets. Once all of the caches have been found and the facts read by each small group, the group reconvenes as a whole. Each small group is given eight pieces of paper with one land deal written on each of the pieces of paper. One member of each small group steps forward with the eight pieces of paper. You should then read individual facts aloud about specific land deals. As you read each fact aloud, the representatives for each small group hold up the sheet of paper identifying the land deal they think matches the fact. Points are tallied for correct answers as members of each small group take turns responding to the land deal facts. The small groups compete to see which group correctly identifies the greatest number of facts.

FIGURE 7.11

WESTWARD EXPANSION FACTS

Northwest Territory	Year of acquisition—1783 Country acquired from; method of acquisition—Great Britain; Treaty of Paris President—none Current U.S. states in the acquired land—Ohio, Indiana, Illinois, Michigan, Wisconsin, and parts of Minnesota
Louisiana Territory	Year of acquisition—1803 Country acquired from; method of acquisition—France; purchased President—Thomas Jefferson Current U.S. states in the acquired land—Arkansas, Missouri, Iowa, Oklahoma, Kansas, Nebraska, and parts of Minnesota, North Dakota, South Dakota, New Mexico, Montana, Wyoming, Colorado, and Louisiana
Florida	Year of acquisition—1819 Country acquired from; method of acquisition—Spain; Adams-Onis Treaty President—James Monroe Current U.S. states in the acquired land—Florida
Texas	Year of acquisition—1836 Country acquired from; method of acquisition—Mexico; Texas Revolution President—Andrew Jackson Current U.S. states in the acquired land—Texas
Oregon Territory	Year of acquisition—1846 Country acquired from; method of acquisition—Great Britain; Oregon Treaty President—James Polk Current U.S. states in the acquired land—Oregon, Washington, Idaho, and parts of Montana and Wyoming
Mexican Cession	Year of acquisition—1848 Country acquired from; method of acquisition—Mexico; Mexican War President—James Polk Current U.S. states in the acquired land—Nevada, Utah, and parts of California, Colorado, New Mexico, Arizona, and Wyoming
Gadsden Purchase	Year of acquisition—1853 Country acquired from; method of acquisition—Mexico; purchased President—Franklin Pierce Current U.S. states in the acquired land—parts of Arizona and New Mexico
Alaska	Year of acquisition—1867 Country acquired from; method of acquisition—Russia; purchased President—Andrew Johnson Current U.S. states in the acquired land—Alaska

From J.K. Taylor, D. Kremer, K. Pebworth, and P. Werner, 2010, *Geocaching for schools and communities* (Champaign, IL: Human Kinetics).

ASSESSMENT SUGGESTIONS

✖ Keep track of each small group's correct answers and see which group answers the most facts correctly.

✖ Give small groups a quiz using a format where they match the facts of the land deals with the correct land deals (see figure 7.12).

KEY POINTS

✖ Tell the groups that only one group is allowed at a cache at any given time. If a group finds a cache occupied by another group, they must wait until the first group leaves before they can begin reading the facts.

✖ Map the cache locations and watch for small groups having difficulty in locating the caches. Assist them as needed.

✖ Match weak and strong participants together in small groups to keep the groups even in their ability to recall information.

✖ Make sure all participants take an equal number of turns standing and answering for their small group as they identify the land deal facts.

VARIATIONS

✖ Place hints to each cache's location in sealed envelopes. Give these envelopes to the small groups for them to use if they need help finding the caches. Participants may gain additional points for returning the envelopes unopened at the end of the learning experience.

✖ Distribute a partially blank worksheet to each small group for them to complete based on what they recall from the facts found in the caches. These worksheets could also be completed individually rather than in small groups.

✖ Have the small groups complete a blank worksheet that identifies only the land deals rather than using a partially blank worksheet. These worksheets can also be completed individually rather than in small groups.

✖ Have the small groups complete a worksheet that uses a matching format for the facts. These worksheets can also be completed individually rather than in small groups.

✖ Use a relay format in which students from each small group individually or in pairs take turns locating the caches and reading the facts about the land deals.

✖ Have participants complete the worksheet individually first and then collaborate with their small group for any assistance needed in completing the worksheet.

✖ Alter the learning experience so that each cache contains four unrelated facts about land deals. The small group's assignment would be to correctly link each fact with the appropriate land deal. The group writes the correct answers on their worksheet, which they take from cache to cache until all caches have been found and the worksheet has been completed. This format can also be used for other geographical and historical events.

FIGURE 7.12

WESTWARD EXPANSION QUIZ

Name _____ Teacher _____

Match each land deal with the year it took place.

1. Alaska
2. Florida
3. Gadsden Purchase
4. Louisiana Territory
5. Mexican Cession
6. Northwest Territory
7. Oregon Territory
8. Texas

a. 1783
b. 1803
c. 1819
d. 1836
e. 1846
f. 1848
g. 1853
h. 1867

Match each land deal with the country involved in the deal and how the land was obtained.

1. Alaska
2. Florida
3. Gadsden Purchase
4. Louisiana Territory
5. Mexican Cession
6. Northwest Territory
7. Oregon Territory
8. Texas

a. Great Britain; Treaty of Paris
b. France; purchased
c. Great Britain; Oregon Treaty
d. Mexico; Mexican War
e. Mexico; purchased
f. Mexico; Texas Revolution
g. Spain; Adams-Onis Treaty
h. Russia; purchased

From J.K. Taylor, D. Kremer, K. Pebworth, and P. Werner, 2010, *Geocaching for schools and communities* (Champaign, IL: Human Kinetics).

Match each land deal with the president who was in office when the land deal occurred.

1. Alaska

2. Florida

3. Gadsden Purchase

4. Louisiana Territory

5. Mexican Cession

6. Northwest Territory

7. Oregon Territory

8. Texas

a. none (there was no president yet)

b. Andrew Jackson

c. Thomas Jefferson

d. Andrew Johnson

e. James Monroe

f. Franklin Pierce

g. James Polk

h. James Polk

Match each land deal with the states that were created from the land deal.

1. Alaska

2. Florida

3. Gadsden Purchase

4. Louisiana Territory

5. Mexican Cession

6. Northwest Territory

7. Oregon Territory

8. Texas

a. Alaska

b. Arkansas, Missouri, Iowa, Oklahoma, Kansas, Nebraska, and parts of other states

c. Florida

d. Nevada, Utah, and parts of other states

e. Ohio, Indiana, Illinois, Michigan, Wisconsin, and parts of Minnesota

f. Oregon, Washington, Idaho, and parts of other states

g. parts of Arizona and New Mexico

h. Texas

From J.K. Taylor, D. Kremer, K. Pebworth, and P. Werner, 2010, *Geocaching for schools and communities* (Champaign, IL: Human Kinetics).

Social Studies 2

State of the Union

CONTENT AREA
Geography—state capitals and large cities in the United States

OVERVIEW
Participants will locate the capital of each state and cities within a given state that have populations greater than 20,000 people. They will create a map of the state and locate those cities on the map. Participants will also map the top 10 most populated cities on a map of the United States.

OBJECTIVES
By participating in this learning experience, participants will improve their ability to do the following:

✖ Identify the most populated cities in the United States.

✖ Identify state capitals in the United States.

✖ Identify the geographical locations of major cities and state capitals in the United States.

EQUIPMENT
GPS units (one per small group), enough cache containers to place several state capitals in each container, state capitals written on individually numbered slips of paper, pencils, an answer sheet, a computer, access to the Internet, outlines of U.S. state maps (try looking for these at www.eduplace.com/ss/maps/states.html), and an outline of a map of the United States (try looking for this at www.eduplace.com/ss/maps/usa.html)

ORGANIZATION
This learning experience alternates between large-group activity, small-group activity, and individual work, beginning and ending as a large-group activity. Before the learning experience, access the geocaching.com Web site to become familiar with the Web pages used for this learning experience. On the geocaching.com Web site, select Hide & Seek a Cache from the navigation bar on the left side of the page. Under Seek a Cache, choose a state from the By State Page drop-down menu. The page that appears will include a drop-down menu of cities within the state that have populations of at least 20,000 people. These cities will be used for the learning experience. Also write each state capital on an individually numbered slip of paper. Each cache will contain several numbered state capitals. The number of state capitals in each cache is determined by the number of caches created. If 10 caches are created, each cache would contain 5 state capitals. Once the caches have been created, hide them and record the coordinates of their locations. The coordinates for each hidden cache must then be uploaded into the GPS units. Upload the

coordinates into the GPS units yourself or teach the participants how to do this as part of the learning experience.

DESCRIPTION

With the entire group, discuss the 10 cities in the United States with the largest populations (see figure 7.13). Working as one large group or in small groups, have participants use resources such as almanacs, road maps, atlases, and the Internet to locate those 10 cities on an outline map of the United States.

Next, divide the participants into small groups and show them how to use the geocaching.com Web site to identify cities in a state that have populations over 20,000. Assign a different state to each small group. Have group members work together on a computer to locate the information for their state on the geocaching.com Web site. Give each small group a copy of the map of their state and have them locate the cities on their map. The state capital and its population should also be identified for each state. Once the participants have completed the assignment, which may require several sessions, the whole group reconvenes. Participants can then report on the state capital and cities in their states with large populations.

Next, explain the use of GPS units and latitude and longitude coordinates as a way to pinpoint specific locations anywhere in the world. If a geocache is

---

FIGURE 7.13

TOP 10 LARGEST CITIES IN THE UNITED STATES BY POPULATION

1. New York City—8,363,710
2. Los Angeles—3,833,995
3. Chicago—2,853,114
4. Houston—2,242,193
5. Phoenix—1,567,924
6. Philadelphia—1,447,395
7. San Antonio—1,351,305
8. Dallas—1,279,910
9. San Diego—1,279,329
10. San Jose—948,279

From www.census.gov/newsroom/releases/pdf/cb09-99_city_growth_2008a.pdf.

located close by, show the geocache and its coordinates to the group using the geocaching.com Web site. Then explain that a certain number of caches have been hidden in the area that contain the capitals of the United States. Tell the participants that their assignment is to use the GPS units to locate the caches and identify the state associated with each state capital inside each cache. Each state capital is numbered and the participants should write down the state associated with each numbered state capital.

Divide the participants into small groups and show them how to access the cache coordinates in the GPS unit. Send the participants out with a blank numbered answer sheet to locate the caches and identify and record the states by their capitals. Groups can reconvene as one large group at the end of the learning experience, determine the number of correctly identified states, and compete against each other to see who identified the greatest number of states correctly.

ASSESSMENT SUGGESTIONS

✖ Have participants turn in their state maps with the cities indicated so that the maps can be checked for accuracy.

✖ From information shared by the participants, create a quiz that requires the participants to match each city to its appropriate state.

✖ From information shared by the participants, create a quiz that requires the participants to match the state capitals to their respective states. Have participants identify which state capitals have populations greater than 20,000.

✖ Assign states to each participant, and have them investigate that state individually and report their findings to the group.

✖ Have participants turn in their answer sheets so they can be checked for accuracy.

KEY POINTS

✖ Create a master map of the cache locations and watch for small groups having difficulty in locating the caches. Assist them as needed.

✖ Watch for small groups and individual participants who are having trouble negotiating through the Web pages on geocaching.com. Assist them as needed.

✖ Watch for small groups and individual participants who are having difficulty locating resources that show the cities in their state. Assist them as needed.

✖ Watch for small groups and individual participants who are not staying on task when working on the computer. Monitor the computer screens to make sure everyone stays on task.

VARIATIONS

✖ Place hints to each cache's location in sealed envelopes. Give these envelopes to the small groups for them to use if they need help finding the caches. Participants may gain additional points for returning the envelopes unopened at the end of the learning experience.

✖ Expand the learning experience to include an investigation of the state's topography as well as other pertinent information. This information could include the state population, the number of representatives for the state, the governor of the state, when the state entered the union, the industry of the state, the state flag, the state bird, the state tree, the state flower, and so on.

✖ Have participants investigate key events that occurred in the state related to the history of the United States. Influential people born in the state can also be identified.

Suggested Additional Learning Experiences

Following are suggestions for additional learning experiences. For each of the ideas, a name and a short description are provided to get you started in developing more lessons that integrate geocaching with disciplinary subjects. The sky is the limit. Good luck!

Language Arts 1: The Path Less Traveled

Within a poetry unit in English, have several groups of participants each hide a cache that contains a poem from their favorite poet but with the poet's name missing. After the cache coordinates have been uploaded to GPS units, fellow participants locate the caches and correctly identify as many poets as possible. As an alternative, the group as a whole or in small groups can create a cache or caches, and each participant then writes a description of the cache in a specific poem form such as haiku. The group votes on which description they like best for each cache and uses that description for the cache. The cache can then be submitted to geocaching.com for approval and can be hidden for other geocachers to find. Have participants monitor the cache to see how many times it is found.

Language Arts 2: History Mystery

Find a location such as a school, recreation center, or community center. Have participants write a short history about the location. The short history should be informative and relevant, should contain facts, and should be written using grammatically correct language. A traditional cache can then be created with the history included as part of the cache's description and the cache can be submitted to geocaching.com for approval and hidden for other geocachers to find. Have participants monitor the cache to see how many times it is found.

Mathematics 1: Route 66—Where Are You?

Have participants read about Route 66, the highway from Chicago to Los Angeles. For historical and road information about Route 66, you can visit two Web sites: www.theroadwanderer.net/route66.htm and www.historic66.com. The original route was 2,451 miles in length (www.missouri66.org/history.html; see figure 7.14 for a state-by-state breakdown of its length). However, as towns were bypassed by interstate systems and the end of the route was moved from Los Angeles to Santa Monica, the length of the route decreased to 2,278 miles.

After a discussion of the historical significance of Route 66, participants can enter the coordinates of cities and towns along the original and along the newer Route 66 and calculate the mileage from their current location to those cities and towns. Next, participants can calculate how much gas money it would take to travel from their current location to these various

---

FIGURE 7.14

ROUTE 66 FROM CHICAGO, ILLINOIS, TO LOS ANGELES, CALIFORNIA

	Route 66 mileage in 1926
Illinois	301
Missouri	317
Kansas	13
Oklahoma	432
Texas	186
New Mexico	487
Arizona	401
California	314
Total	2,451

cities and towns along the entire Route 66 distance if they traveled at an average speed of 60 miles per hour in a vehicle that gets 25 miles to the gallon with gas priced at $2.75 per gallon. To make the problem more complex, participants could investigate the average price of gas for each state that Route 66 passes through and calculate the total cost of gas for a trip based on gas costs for each individual state. A Web site to determine current gas prices is www.fuelgaugereport.com.

Mathematics 2: It IS a Numbers Game!

Create caches that require participants to use math skills to determine the cache coordinates. Math problems from any unit that the participants are studying can be used to generate numbers for determining cache coordinates. Small groups of participants can race to solve the problems and determine the coordinates.

For example, provide the participants with a math problem that, when solved, generates a two-digit answer. Designate one digit as a and the other as b. Then give the participants cache coordinates in which they must replace a and b with the two digits.

Example: N 37° 24.34<u>a</u>, W 079° 09.<u>bb</u>5

Upload cache coordinates into GPS units in advance—one set of cache coordinates for each GPS unit. When the participants solve the coordinates for a cache, check their coordinates for accuracy. If the coordinates are correct, give the group the appropriate GPS unit that has those cache coordinates uploaded; the small group then goes to search for the cache. You may want to put a token item in the cache for the small group to collect as proof of locating the cache. Once the cache has been found, the small group returns as quickly as possible and begins solving another math problem for a different hidden cache. Once the next math problem has been solved—and the cache coordinates have been determined and checked for accuracy—the small group again uses the appropriate GPS unit to search for the cache.

During the learning experience, small groups might find themselves in a situation where they have the correct coordinates but the GPS unit containing those coordinates is being used by another group. Rather than simply waiting for the GPS unit to be returned, the group might strategically begin solving math problems for the other hidden caches in order to determine those cache coordinates. Then the waiting group would be ahead of the other groups in determining the correct coordinates for all of the hidden caches.

To make this experience more difficult, use more complex math problems, or create math problems that result in three or four numbers that would be used to determine the cache coordinates. Another option is to let the participants create their own math problems and cache coordinates; they can then hide caches for each other at those coordinates.

Science 1: CITO

Geocachers are often interested in ecology and the environment. Across the United States, events known as Cache In Trash Out (CITO) have been organized by local geocaching clubs to clean up the litter found in rivers, lakes, parks, and other areas of concern. Usually, trash bags are provided, and geocachers gather together for a morning, afternoon, or whole day of work to clean up an area that has been littered. During these gatherings, the geocachers may also bring food to share for a meal and maybe even hunt a few caches in the area after the cleanup is completed. Find a CITO event in your area and challenge participants as individuals, in small groups, or as a large group to participate in the event to help clean up the environment. If there are no CITO events in your area, plan your own CITO event to clean up the local school grounds or a local park or recreation area. Announce the event online to fellow cachers and provide bags to be used during the trash pickup. Discuss with the group how long it takes for different types of trash to biodegrade and how recycling is one way to dispose of trash responsibly. Help save the environment!

Science 2: The Shinbone's Connected to What?

To reinforce the study of bones in the human body, create caches that are large enough to contain bones that the participants should be able to identify by shape. Place several bones in each cache; then hide the caches and upload the cache coordinates to GPS units. Participants then use the GPS units to locate the caches and identify the bones contained in each cache. Number the caches and give the participants a worksheet to fill in as they find the numbered caches. Check each participant's worksheet for accuracy when they have finished to assess their knowledge of the bones of the body.

Social Studies 1 (History): What's Happening?

Use the geocaching.com Web site to locate historical geocaches in the local area. Take participants on a field trip to find these geocaches. After the geocaching excursion, have participants investigate the history highlighted in the caches in greater detail using their textbooks, resources in the library, or information from the Internet. If there are no historical caches in the local area, have participants investigate local history at a nearby cemetery, park, museum, statue, or marker. After investigating the history, participants can use that history to create a traditional cache or multicache. The cache can then be submitted to geocaching.com for approval and can be hidden for other geocachers to find. Have participants monitor the cache to see how many times it is found.

Social Studies 2 (History): I Remember When . . .

Visit www.nps.gov/history/NR/twhp/descrip.htm to obtain readings and lesson plans for historic sites. Lesson plans can be browsed by national standards for history or by curriculum standards for social studies. You can access specific lesson plans from the Web site based on the content area to be studied. In addition, the site provides questions for participants to answer after completing the readings.

Create several caches; each cache should contain multiple copies of a single reading (figure 7.15). Hide the caches and upload the coordinates into GPS units. Give participants a worksheet that contains the questions for each reading. Participants can complete the worksheets individually or as a small group as they locate the caches. To assess the participants' understanding of the readings, check the worksheets for accuracy at the end of the learning experience.

Social Studies 3 (Geography): Where's Who?

After reading or learning about a specific site or location, participants can use a Web site such as http://itouchmap.com/latlong.html to determine the latitude and longitude coordinates of the location. Have the participants upload the coordinates into a GPS unit. Using the Go To feature of the GPS unit, participants determine how far the location is from their current location. Have the participants estimate how long it would take to arrive at that location if they could travel in a straight line between the two points by foot, bicycle, or car. Then have the participants use a Web site such as MapQuest (www.mapquest.com) to determine the driving mileage between the two sites. Next, have participants re-estimate how long it would take them to travel between the two points by foot, bicycle, or car using the distance from the driving directions. Conduct a group discussion about possible reasons why the roads and highways were built where they were rather than in a straight line between two points. You may want to use topography and terrain maps during this discussion.

Social Studies 4 (Geography): Coordinate This!

Identify latitude and longitude coordinates of specific locations (cities, states, or countries) for the participants to investigate. To identify coordinates for specific locations, you may visit http://itouchmap.com/latlong.html. Record the coordinates in degrees, minutes, and seconds. Assign coordinates to individual participants or small groups of students. The participants can use the same Web site and enter the coordinates to discover their assigned location. Have participants investigate the location and prepare a report of their investigation. Topics will vary depending on the unit being covered, but participants might report on topographical features, climate, crops, livestock, indigenous plants and animals, bordering states or countries, or waterways. Participants may also enter the coordinates of their assigned location into a GPS unit and determine how many miles away the assigned location is from their present position.

FIGURE 7.15

READING EXAMPLE AND QUESTIONS

Three Days of Carnage at Gettysburg

Units of the Union and the Confederate armies met near Gettysburg on June 30, 1863, and each quickly requested reinforcements. The main battle opened on July 1, with early morning attacks by the Confederates on Union troops on McPherson Ridge, west of the town. Though outnumbered, the Union forces held their position. The fighting escalated throughout the day as more soldiers from each army reached the battle area. By 4 p.m., the Union troops were overpowered, and they retreated through the town, where many were quickly captured. The remnants of the Union force fell back to Cemetery Hill and Culp's Hill, south of town. The Southerners failed to pursue their advantage, however, and the Northerners labored long into the night regrouping their men.

Throughout the night, both armies moved their men to Gettysburg and took up positions in preparation for the next day. By the morning of July 2, the main strength of both armies had arrived on the field. Battle lines were drawn up in sweeping arcs similar to a "J," or fishhook shape. The main portions of both armies were nearly a mile apart on parallel ridges: Union forces on Cemetery Ridge, Confederate forces on Seminary Ridge, to the west. General Robert E. Lee, commanding the Confederate troops, ordered attacks against the Union left and right flanks (ends of the lines). Starting in late afternoon, Confederate General James Longstreet's attacks on the Union left made progress, but they were checked by Union reinforcements brought to the fighting from the Culp's Hill area and other uncontested parts of the Union battle line. To the north, at the bend and barb of the fishhook (the other flank), Confederate General Richard Ewell launched his attack in the evening as the fighting at the other end of the fishhook was subsiding. Ewell's men seized part of Culp's Hill, but elsewhere they were repulsed. The day's results were indecisive for both armies.

In the very early morning of July 3, the Union army forced out the Confederates who had successfully taken Culp's Hill the previous evening. Then General Lee, having attacked the ends of the Union line the previous day, decided to assail the Union. The attack was preceded by a two-hour artillery bombardment of Cemetery Hill and Ridge. For a time, the massed guns of both armies were engaged in a thunderous duel for supremacy. The Union defensive position held. In a final attempt to gain the initiative and win the

From J.K. Taylor, D. Kremer, K. Pebworth, and P. Werner, 2010, *Geocaching for schools and communities* (Champaign, IL: Human Kinetics). Adapted from the National Park Service's visitor's guide for Gettysburg National Military Park. From: www.nps.gov/history/NR/twhp/wwwlps/lessons/44gettys/44facts1.htm.

battle, Lee sent approximately 12,000 soldiers across the one mile of open fields that separated the two armies near the Union center. General George Meade, commander of the Union forces, anticipated such a move and had readied his army. The Union lines did not break. Only every other Southerner who participated in this action retired to safety. Despite great courage, the attack (sometimes called Pickett's Charge or Longstreet's assault) was repulsed with heavy losses. Crippled by extremely heavy casualties in the three days at Gettysburg, the Confederates could no longer continue the battle, and on July 4 they began to withdraw from Gettysburg.

1. Which army had the advantage after the first day of fighting? What were some reasons for their success? Could they have been even more successful?

2. What was the situation by the evening of July 2?

3. What evidence from the previous day's fighting brought General Lee to decide on the strategy for Pickett's Charge on July 3? What was the result of that assault?

4. Why did General Lee decide to withdraw from Gettysburg?

From J.K. Taylor, D. Kremer, K. Pebworth, and P. Werner, 2010, *Geocaching for schools and communities* (Champaign, IL: Human Kinetics). Adapted from the National Park Service's visitor's guide for Gettysburg National Military Park. From: www.nps.gov/history/NR/twhp/wwwlps/lessons/44gettys/44facts1.htm.

DEVELOPING A GEOCACHING PROGRAM

As the preceding chapters have outlined, geocaching is an activity that can serve a variety of purposes. People working anywhere in education or leisure and recreation can use geocaching to provide social, educational, and physical activity benefits to their participants. Geocaching will offer different benefits in different settings. In some settings, integrating geocaching will be easy, and the benefits will be obvious. In other settings, the integration of geocaching will require some creative thinking. Perhaps your interest has been piqued and you are considering ways to integrate geocaching into your class or programs, but the task seems somewhat onerous. This chapter is intended to help you get started. For some, the goal may be to develop a geocaching club or ongoing program; others may be looking to create a short unit of instruction or perhaps a solitary experience. Regardless of your particular application of geocaching, the sense of adventure and intrinsic reward of finding a prize at the end of a challenging search can capture the participants' imagination, stimulate their interest, and turn them on to your message.

This chapter provides a suggested progression of activities—from simple to complex—that might be used to integrate geocaching into a variety of educational, recreational, and leisure settings. For those who do not have access to the GPS units required for traditional geocaching, the following progression suggests a series of low-tech experiences that would not require the use of GPS units. After exploring ways to introduce simple geocaching experiences without GPS units, this chapter presents ideas and suggestions designed to help you raise new funds to acquire the requisite technology to integrate geocaching more completely into your programs.

Integrating Geocaching

Regardless of the context in which you are working, integrating geocaching into the activities that you use with your participants does not need to be overly time consuming or labor intensive. You could start by jumping in with a few new introductory experiences to test your own skills and resolve, or you could integrate geocaching or a low-tech alternative into something else that you are already doing. Starting any extensive new program can take time; however, geocaching is an activity that you can ease into by starting with some of the lead-up, low-tech alternatives that have been presented in this book. The diagram in figure 8.1 illustrates a progression of learning experiences that could be used to gradually introduce geocaching in either recreational or education settings. This progression might be particularly valuable if the leader or organizer has no familiarity or background experience with geocaching.

Letterboxing provides an ideal way to begin a geocaching unit or program. With letterboxing, there is no need to invest in expensive equipment,

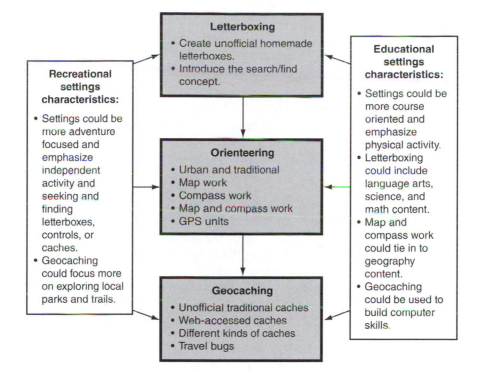

X Figure 8.1 Progression for introducing geocaching.

and you don't even need special skills or experience. As a simple starting point, you may use a progression of letterboxes that participants visit in sequence to complete a course. The course of letterboxes could be creatively structured to lead participants toward a particular objective. For example, if you are a teacher covering U.S. history and you want to teach students about the original 13 colonies, you could begin by hiding 13 letterboxes around the school campus. Armed with a clipboard, a worksheet, a pencil, clues, and a compass, students set off to locate the letterboxes in sequence. You can have different groups of students start at different points in order to spread the groups out. Students discover the name of an original colony in every letterbox they find. Each letterbox is named for a particular colony and may include additional interesting facts or information about that colony. A unique stamp could also be provided in each letterbox; students can use this stamp to mark their worksheet and prove that they visited that letterbox. In this or any similar activity, participants will be problem solving and working together with others while being physically active. In addition, they will be having fun.

You don't need to list your letterboxes online unless you want this to be part of the learning experience for participants. Indeed, if you want to post the letterboxes, the participants may list them online for you as part of their participation. Be responsible though—if you list a geocache or a letterbox online, then you are responsible for maintaining the cache for as long as it is posted on the applicable Web site. If you have participants list a letterbox or geocache as part of a program or unit of instruction, you should remind them of their responsibilities in terms of maintaining the cache until they remove it from the online listings.

If your objectives call for sharing informational or instructional materials, then letterboxes could include themes or provide clues that participants must research individually or in groups. The learning experiences described in the preceding chapters contain specific ideas about how to use geocaching activities to cover various content areas. These ideas could easily be adapted for a letterboxing activity. If letterboxing is where you begin, your overall objectives may ultimately determine the most appropriate next step. However, orienteering would be an ideal activity to use after letterboxing.

Orienteering is a great way to get kids and adults running and walking without them getting bored or worried about how far they're going. Physical education teachers can set up a number of urban courses and use them as warm-ups or training activities before a mile run or other fitness test. Recreation professionals can use orienteering to help people explore their local parks and improve their map-reading skills. Whatever the setting, orienteering can be a great lead-up activity to geocaching because it has many similar facets.

After an introduction to letterboxing and orienteering, your participants should be ready to begin geocaching. As suggested earlier in this book, you can begin geocaching even before you have a GPS unit. This may be a necessary first step if you don't have access to GPS units. If you are going to try geocaching without a GPS unit, you still need to have access to the Internet. You will need to print out caches, along with an accompanying map of their location, from the geocaching.com Web site. With detailed printouts of the cache and its

TRAIL TALE

Kevin

One way to inspire groups to have fun or to become more interested in geocaching is through the use of travel bugs. A colleague of ours who's a college professor once divided his class into two teams, designating one the American League and one the National League. At the start of the semester, each team had to create a travel bug whose mission was to visit all the baseball parks in its assigned league. The teams placed their travel bugs in a geocache and listed the bugs on the geocaching.com Web site, asking people to send them a digital image of the travel bug in front of one of the appropriate major-league ballparks. The team whose travel bug visited the most ballparks in the assigned league by the end of the semester was the winner.

location, you can begin caching with a very high probability of success even if you don't have a GPS.

At some point, for you to fully introduce geocaching, your participants will need access to a handheld GPS unit. Initially, people can easily share a GPS, and they certainly do not each need their own unit. Although GPS units are becoming more commonplace, the fact remains that GPS units are not cheap, especially when you are trying to buy a set of them for a class. Depending on your situation, you may be able to have the participants buy or borrow their own units. In settings where you are working with adults, this would undoubtedly be the way to go. If participants don't have a GPS, they may have a mobile phone on which they can download a geocaching application to make the phone perform like a GPS unit. As discussed earlier, geocaching applications for smart phones are becoming increasingly prevalent.

As you start to introduce geocaching, your most valuable asset will be a sound knowledge of the area where you are going to be working. If you are going to have people moving around in a given area searching for caches, you need to be aware of any safety hazards, the common paths of travel, and the nature of the terrain. In an instructional setting, one of the best ways to begin is with small groups of students moving through a pre-planned course and visiting a certain number of caches in a predetermined sequence. With this method, you can control—to some degree—where and when the students are moving. You can plan the course to avoid roads, busy thoroughfares, and environmentally delicate or sensitive areas.

In the early stages of teaching geocaching, the best plan is to use caches that you set yourself for the purpose of the class; these are caches that you will not publish on the geocaching.com Web site. This way, you can steer the caching more easily to help your participants improve, and you can include any other content that is important to your setting. Start with traditional caches that are large and easy to find. Then gradually increase the complexity of caches by moving to smaller, well-hidden caches. Hiding multiple caches for participants to find during instruction can be time consuming; however, once the locations are planned out, the setup time is reduced, and the students can collect the caches as they go so that you don't have to collect them after the activity. As your group progresses, you can assign small groups of students the task of hiding a cache for other students to find. This format can lead to some fun instructional sessions as teams vie to make their cache the best or the most difficult to find.

When introducing geocaching, you need to find an area with a clear view of the sky so that the GPS units will work well. Students who are learning how to use a GPS unit will quickly get frustrated if the GPS unit is constantly giving them a warning message that it is "searching for satellites." In addition, some of your participants may be intimidated by the

✖ Beginning geocachers can set caches for each other to find as they learn to use the GPS in hunting for a geocache.

new technology when they are first introduced to a handheld GPS unit. Helping these participants get to a point where they are comfortable with the GPS unit will be one of your biggest challenges. Try to avoid lecturing on how to use the GPS. Using a GPS tends to be fairly intuitive, and students will understand your explanations a great deal more if they have some hands-on experience. Through a progression of finding gradually more challenging caches, participants should develop their ability to use the GPS fairly quickly. Peer teaching works well when people are first learning how to use a GPS. You can easily facilitate this by pairing students and having them share one GPS unit. By completing the activities together, the participants can take turns being in charge of the GPS unit, and they can help each other understand the nuances of the device.

After participants have progressed through the process of hiding and finding caches with gradually increasing levels of complexity, you may be looking for a way to keep the participants motivated. A great way to do this is to hold a series of sessions in which two teams set caches for the other team to find. Each session can have different requirements for the type of cache, or the teams may set a series of caches, creating a course to be completed by the other team. A series of hide-and-find sessions such as this can provide a fun way for students to build their skills in using the GPS as well as in hiding and finding caches.

After covering the basics of geocaching, try to provide an activity that will help participants see how geocaching can transfer to their life outside of your class or program. This could be as simple as having people visit a cache as part of a trip they are taking for business or pleasure. Field trips are also great for this purpose. You could meet your group at a local state or county park to visit existing caches or to hide and seek your own. In a growing number of communities, groups of geocachers periodically gather for event caches, which would also make an excellent experience for your geocaching unit. Event caches have the added benefit of connecting experienced geocachers with those who are just learning. Your local event caches will be listed on the geocaching.com Web site. Subscribing to the Web site's weekly e-mail newsletter will also help you stay up to date on new event caches in your area.

Using Geocaching in the Leisure and Tourism Industry

If you work in the leisure and tourism industry, you should consider the potential that geocaching might offer in this industry. The activities organized by the Maryland Municipal League (cited in the Trail Tale on p. 186) are just one example of a group using geocaching to draw people into their state. The chamber of commerce headquarters in Salt Lake City has a travel bug hotel. Visitors can take a travel bug from the bug hotel (or they can leave a bug there), and these travel bugs help people find out about geocaches in Salt Lake City. Geocaching in Salt Lake City will quickly help you discover where Brigham Young is buried and many other interesting facts about how the Mormons established the city. Geocaching in Little Rock, Arkansas, very quickly yields many interesting facts about Native Americans, the British, and battles that took place in the founding of that city. In short, geocaching can turn history into action!

The parks and recreation department on Jekyll Island, Georgia, has a number of GPS units that you can rent for the day to find caches on the island while you are out and about. You can bike or walk to find a number of caches. By locating the caches, you also find out interesting facts, including history about the Rockefellers and information about lighthouses, sea turtles, fun parks, and other island attractions. At the park headquarters, you can check out a GPS unit and get a map and a list of caches with over 10 caches to find on one island. More frequently, state parks are setting and maintaining caches that are specifically intended to attract people to the park. For example, in Sesquicentennial State Park in Columbia, South Carolina, there are over 10 caches designed to draw people into the park. By downloading the coordinates, groups could spend an entire day in the park walking or biking to find each of the caches—while doing so, these people will also be socializing with friends, getting exercise, finding treasures, and learning new facts about the area.

Kevin

In a particularly creative example of using geocaching to promote travel and tourism, the Maryland Municipal League (MML) challenged visitors to find geocaches throughout the state of Maryland. The MML is a statewide nonprofit organization that represents 157 municipal governments to advocate for and strengthen municipal government in the state. The MML geocaching trail covers 78 towns and cities throughout 11 specially designated districts. The MML offered a limited edition coin to the first 500 people who visited at least two of the cache sites in each of the 11 districts. Geocache trail passports were made available at participating county visitor centers; in these passports, participating geocachers collected a stamp and wrote down a unique code word (Palk, 2008).

When people first start geocaching, they are often amazed to find out how many geocaches are hidden in the area where they live. There are now so many geocaches in the United States that the average American most likely passes by at least one cache when traveling to school, work, or the local grocery store. Indeed, if that journey takes as much as 30 minutes, then the person is likely to pass a great many more! The fact that people regularly travel past geocaches without knowing the caches are there makes it all the more intriguing to many people when they first begin geocaching. People are commonly surprised at finding so many geocaches close to their home, and they are also surprised at the things they learn about their local surroundings. They might learn interesting historical facts that they didn't know. They might discover a new trail that they had no idea was there or that they simply never found time to walk. Or they might discover something as simple as a view or vantage point that they pause at for the first time while geocaching. Geocaching makes people look for things—and when they really start looking, many people find things they had never seen before. People lead busy lives, and they tend to move through their local environment without looking around very carefully or thoroughly. When the same people start hunting for something in that same area, they look at it in a wholly different way and are often surprised by what they find.

Gathering Support to Start a Program

With resources increasingly scarce and uncertain economic times ahead, new programs and equipment often require grant writing and fund-raising activities. Although many recreation departments and YMCA programs are used to fund-raising for new programs, school teachers are often less well prepared. Teacher education programs don't usually include a class on fund-raising, and teachers often become involved in fund-raising

✖ Finding your first geocache can be a lot of fun.

activities with little appreciation for the necessary skills. Some school districts provide support to teachers who are looking to raise funds, and the district office would undoubtedly be a great place to start for many teachers. Some districts employ grant writers to help the already busy principals and teachers; these grant writers will also be a great resource if they are available to you.

If you are new to fund-raising or grant writing, don't be intimidated; start small and learn as you go. An absolute necessity is to start with a clear sense of exactly what you are trying to accomplish. If you are going to write a grant proposal, your first step is to write a clear statement of your goals and needs. This will help you pinpoint exactly what you need and may ultimately help you identify where you might look for support. Armed with a clear statement of your goals, you can begin to look for people in your local community whom you might collaborate with.

Grant Writing

For many teachers, a stigma is attached to grant writing—the sense that it will take someone away from teaching and that it's very challenging. Many believe that writing a grant proposal is not something that is achievable for the average teacher. The reality is that writing a grant proposal does not have to fit those stereotypes. Depending on the funding agency that is offering the grant, the requirements for people making applications can vary greatly. Larger grant proposals are a great deal of work to prepare, but you do not need a large grant to start a geocaching unit or program. If you are interested in large state or federal grants, then you should be aware that the proposals involve an extensive writing process and are best written by professional grant writers working with a well-organized team of professionals. A proposal for a large grant will need to focus on far more than the introduction of geocaching into your curriculum, and there are a myriad of smaller potential funding agencies that require no more than a carefully written letter or a 500-word proposal.

A surprisingly large number of small funding agencies—including small family foundations—provide grants of a few thousand dollars at a time, which may be ideal for someone starting a program. You can perform Internet searches focused on your state, your local area, and key words such as *education, physical activity, foundation, grant,* or *philanthropy.* This type of search will often yield a surprising number of possibilities. Obviously, results will vary greatly between different states and different communities, but this kind of search is always a good place to start. Your local library or local better business bureau is also a great place to begin. When looking for support within your community, the issue of where that support might come from will depend on the unique structure of your local community. The best advice to people searching for local support might simply be to engage in and study their community.

Community Support

A growing number of communities in the United States now have some form of community foundation. A community foundation is designed to pool charitable donations into a coordinated investment fund that provides grants and is dedicated to the social improvement of the community. In more rural areas, the typical community foundation will cover a larger geographical area and may serve the people of one or more counties covering a number of small towns. The typical grant application for a local community foundation is brief and to the point, somewhere in the region of 500 to 1,000 words maximum. Read the instructions carefully; grants of this nature are often reviewed by volunteers with limited time. A poorly formatted submission that doesn't follow the prescribed guidelines is likely to be quickly weeded out!

Community foundations may be a resource even if they do not have a grant available. These foundations can be a tremendous resource in identifying other sources of support. Some may even provide assistance in the preparation of a funding request. Community foundations are strongly focused on connecting with community members who are able to support nonprofits either by providing funds or supporting those applying for funds. A community foundation may be able to help you connect with people in your community who could volunteer to help or could provide access to facilities, resources, or equipment. Even if you don't have a community foundation in your area, you may be able to create your own community support network by reaching out to community members affected by your work.

If you are running a geocaching unit within a school or youth recreation program, you may find parents or other people within the organization who can help raise funds or write a grant. You should consider the obvious potential collaborators, such as the parents of children you are working with. However, you should also think broadly about others who are unique to your organization, such as board members, parishioners, donors, or retired workers who may have technical writing skills. In addition to grant writing, community collaborators may be able to help by establishing support networks and making connections with any local philanthropists who could support your needs.

One of the most powerful and mutually beneficial fund-raising concepts is the tax deduction given to businesses and individuals who support non-profit organizations. This is an important avenue to consider for anyone raising funds, but you need to be aware of the procedures associated with establishing tax-exempt status. Organizations that are not profit driven, such as schools, are not automatically eligible to receive tax-deductible donations of money or any other goods or services. For the donation to be tax deductible in the United States, the organization receiving the donation must be classified as a 501(c)(3) tax-exempt organization, a classification that can only be awarded by the IRS. The application for 501(c)(3) status is lengthy and extremely time consuming, so even if you work for a nonprofit organization, this does not automatically mean that it is a 501(c)(3) organization.

Service Organizations

Service clubs and organizations exist to provide support for worthy causes in their local community, and the start of a geocaching program might well be something that a service club would support. If you work with children or in programs that serve low-income populations, the cost of buying GPS units is one of the biggest initial barriers to introducing geocaching; however, these populations are often targeted for support by service clubs. Even if you don't have to buy GPS units, you may be able to use support from a service club in your local community to enhance your geocaching unit or program through some of the growing number of resources available (for examples of these resources, visit www.educaching.com/educaching.html).

Parent-Teacher Association   For those working in schools in the United States, although the school itself may not be registered as a 501(c)

(3) organization, the school's parent-teacher association (PTA) can serve as the recipient of any tax-deductible donations. The PTA is probably affiliated with a broader, state PTA that is almost certainly a fully tax-exempt organization connected to the national PTA. For this reason—and for many others—the PTA is a great starting point for teachers looking to fund new curriculum projects. Even within a small school district, large variations can exist in the amount of funding available through the PTA of various schools. If a given PTA does not have funds, the organization will generally be able to provide volunteers who can help organize fund-raisers. The PTA is a specifically focused service organization, but there are other community-based service organizations that may be willing to help fund the purchase of equipment to start a geocaching program either in a school or a recreation setting.

Rotary Club   Rotary International is an organization dedicated to service. This organization claims to be the world's first service club and has more than 1.2 million members who volunteer their time and talents to further the Rotary motto of "Service Above Self" (Rotary International, 2010). Communities all over the world are richer for the time, energy, and money provided by hardworking Rotarians who provide generous support in many ways. Regardless of where you are working, if your goal is using geocaching to bring adventure, education, and physical activity to people in your community, you are likely to get support from your local Rotary club. The procedure for requesting support from your local Rotary club will probably involve making a 10- to 15-minute presentation at a lunchtime meeting. Making an attractive handout to support your presentation is always a good idea, although it may not be required. Presenting to your local Rotary club is a simple, straightforward way to solicit support for starting or expanding your geocaching program, and it is well worth the investment of your time.

Lions Club   The Lions Club International claims to be the world's largest service club with over a million members in 45,000 clubs spread across 200 countries throughout the world (Lions Club International,

TRAIL TALE

Peter

While attending a convention in Little Rock, Arkansas, I watched a group of children exiting a school bus and couldn't help but notice that many of the children were carrying GPS units. This was immediately intriguing to me because of my passion for teaching and geocaching, so I asked the staff accompanying the group what they were doing. The group turned out to be from a local private school, and they were conducting a history field trip using geocaching to find out about the history of Little Rock as part of their social studies unit. Each group of students had a series of questions, a map, and a number of caches to find in order to complete their assignment.

2009). Although the Lions clubs have a reputation for tackling large community needs and bigger issues such as providing dental or vision checkups, they are strongly committed to supporting local communities; therefore, asking them for support in getting equipment for your geocaching program is definitely a good idea. If your local Lions club is unable to help you as an organization, the individual members of the club may be motivated to help in various ways. Remember, these are service-oriented members of your local community.

Boys and Girls Clubs   The Boys and Girls Clubs of America are dedicated to providing opportunities for recreation and companionship to children and youth who are unsupervised and who might otherwise be left to their own devices. Boys and Girls Clubs offer programs and services that promote leadership and inclusion and that attempt to build the self-esteem of all participants through a sense of belonging. Their mission is to "enable all young people . . . to reach their full potential as productive, caring, responsible citizens" (Boys and Girls Clubs of America, 2009). In short, the Boys and Girls Clubs are attempting to accomplish the same goals that you might be striving for with a typical geocaching program. Boys and Girls Clubs make a point of reaching out to children and youth who may need them and whose access to extracurricular programming may be limited.

Given the focus of the Boys and Girls Clubs, geocaching would be a wonderful activity to include in an existing program or to establish as a stand-alone program. If you are a geocacher looking to share your hobby and start a program for kids, then the Boys and Girls Clubs could be a great place to house your program. If you are a physical education teacher or a recreation specialist, then you are serving the same population as the Boys and Girls Clubs, and collaborating with your local club might provide the best means of starting a geocaching program.

Collaborating to Start a Program

Collaboration with other like-minded people is always worthwhile; it can provide extra energy, fresh ideas, and an opportunity to share the burden of buying equipment. All communities have schools, so there is an ever present opportunity for collaboration. Collaborating with a school on geocaching does not necessarily have to be tied to physical education. For example, you could collaborate with science teachers on the more technical aspects of a GPS unit. Links between schools and local recreation programs are seldom exploited to their fullest potential. Geocaching programs could be the basis of collaboration between local museums or historical societies, hiking or biking clubs, and schools or parks and recreation departments.

Historically, in the United States at least, physical education has had strong ties to competitive athletic programs, either through the school's athletic department or local community youth sport organizations. In instances where athletic departments do not provide programming, physical education teachers often steer talented players toward youth sport organizations. However, many physical education teachers do not have the same type of direct connection with recreation programs in their community, either at the local parks and recreation department or through organizations such as the Boys and Girls Clubs or the YMCA. Given that geocaching is suitable for people with all levels of ability—rather than only the more talented and physically gifted individuals—the potential for collaboration on geocaching is clearly far greater than for more traditional sport programs. If you are working in parks and recreation, at a Boys and Girls Club, or at a YMCA or YWCA, you should be aware of the potential for collaboration on a geocaching program with any number of teachers in your local schools.

Because physical education is important for all students, not just the physically gifted, physical education teachers should reach out to recreation programs that are open to students of all ability levels. Geocaching is popular in urban areas that are gradually becoming more accessible to people with disabilities; therefore, geocaching could provide an activity that people with and without disabilities can easily complete together. Beyond recommending local programs to students, physical education teachers could reach out to other professionals and coordinate the timing of program offerings and the use of resources such as GPS units. Understandably, some programs will be reluctant to lend out expensive GPS units, but collaboration can work in many ways that don't involve sharing equipment.

School-Based Collaboration in Geocaching

Many secondary schools have programs that allow older students to teach or lead an activity at a neighboring elementary school. These programs foster responsibility and caring on the part of high school students. Programs of this nature are ideal for integrating an activity such as geocaching because the cost of buying materials could be defrayed across the two schools. The high school students could be assigned as mentors to younger students, and the students could work within a buddy system during a supervised and carefully organized geocaching trip within the community. This type of collaboration does not need to be limited solely to the two schools; other community groups and organizations are often happy to support this kind of endeavor. The collaboration might also involve multiple departments within the schools or may be associated with an after-school program.

After-school programs are a great venue for geocaching. After-school programs often have a lot of flexibility in terms of curriculum and schedule, allowing for a great deal of creativity in structuring activities. Parents and others working within an after-school program could set geocaches for you. To help with funding, small grant opportunities are often open to after-school programs (these grants are not applicable to the school's curriculum). Although after-school programs do not affect every child, they often work with some of the more vulnerable and underserved children. For these children, geocaching could represent a wonderful enrichment opportunity. After-school programs are sometimes run with the help of outside agencies such as the local YMCA, parks and recreation department, or Boys and Girls Club. Again, collaboration with these agencies has the potential to be mutually beneficial.

Families

Activities conducted as a family can help parents bond with their kids and can also help keep kids out of trouble! Geocaching is a great family activity because people of different ability levels can participate alongside each other. Whether you are implementing geocaching in a recreation setting or school setting, reaching out to your participants' families and promoting the potential for family involvement will be an important strategy for success.

In many recreation settings, programming is all about providing activities for families, and geocaching has a tremendous amount to offer. Families can be encouraged to use existing parks and facilities by providing opportunities for them to walk or ride bikes to find caches hidden in those areas. Parks and recreation departments might connect with local geocaching groups (through the geocaching.com Web site) to have them set caches that can be promoted through a parks and recreation program. Children will walk remarkable distances without complaint if they are motivated to find a cache that evokes in them a sense of adventure, discovery, and fun. Geocaching families often introduce other families to the activity through the involvement of children. This could provide another fruitful angle that a parks and recreation department can use to focus on family caching.

As families plan activities or vacations together, geocaching can make the experiences more fun and engaging with a focus that has the potential to intrigue the young and old alike. Families and friends can find geocaches while hiking or bicycling on trails near their homes. From trail hikes in Yosemite National Park, to cycling on the Virginia Creeper Trail or the Glacial

Check Your Caches

As a general principle, if you are having participants visit a cache as part of an instructional or introductory experience, you should visit each cache site yourself first. If you have already found the cache yourself, you are better prepared to guide and instruct people who are learning how to geocache.

Drumlin Trail in Wisconsin, families can set out to enjoy an outdoor activity and can increase the incentive level by finding geocaches along the way.

Where are you planning to go on your next family vacation? Why not look up a few caches along the way? Even if you are planning to travel to another country or continent, the global nature of geocaching and the power of Web-based resources (such as Google Earth and Google Maps in concert with the geocaching.com Web site) make it easy to add another layer of interest to your vacation plans. The added layer of interest that geocaching can bring may be a way to get children more interested in discovering aspects of the place you're visiting. As a group activity that is very social, geocaching can certainly help families bond.

Diverse Community Groups

Communities are made stronger by the inclusion of diverse groups with different backgrounds, interests, and motivations. With the large variety of ways that geocaching can be incorporated into other programs and activities, geocaching is a powerful way to bring together diverse community groups. We've already discussed the potential for geocaching to form part of ongoing collaborations between school and recreation programs, after-school programs, city parks and recreation departments, YMCAs, and

✖ Geocaching can include people of all abilities.

community-based initiatives to promote leisure and tourism. Geocaching, perhaps because of its appeal to families, is also a great activity for church groups and youth organizations.

In the same way that geocaching provides powerful bonding experiences for families, it can bring together parishioners of different ages and backgrounds or youth from different elements within a community. A popular activity for church groups is to gather for picnics, cookouts, or potlucks where everyone shares a meal. The potential to combine this kind of activity with geocaching is clearly apparent. Gatherings of any kind where people of diverse backgrounds come together are more enjoyable and engaging when there is a shared activity in which everyone can participate. Geocaching can provide just such an activity.

Conclusion: All Together Now

Developing any new program takes time. Beyond the initial time invested in planning and preparation, the inevitable refining and fine-tuning also take time. But a geocaching program does not need to be labor intensive once the initial planning is in place, and the workload can easily be shared if you think creatively about people and groups whom you might collaborate with. A well-organized set of planning materials for your geocaching activities can be easy to maintain and reuse time and again, making the initial investment all the more worthwhile.

Although insufficient time is often cited as a reason for not implementing a geocaching program, the most common reason is the cost of buying GPS units. These are both legitimate challenges, but neither of them is insurmountable. As previously discussed, many low-tech alternatives can be used as introductory activities, and the basic concepts can be covered without the use of a GPS unit. Once you have the participants hooked on the basics of this exciting activity, there are many ways to elicit support from your local community in order to secure the GPS units needed to build a great geocaching program.

For the authors of this book, one of the most exciting elements of geocaching is that we meet so many interesting people while we're out hunting for caches. You never know whom you're going to bump into while ferreting around for a difficult-to-find geocache. Maybe sometime we'll bump into one of you!

GLOSSARY

aerobic activity—Activity that requires the muscles to use oxygen for energy.

azimuth—A horizontal angle between the vector from an observer to a point of interest and the reference vector (north-south line).

benchmark—A survey marker placed by the National Geodetic Survey.

Cache In Trash Out (CITO)—A program started by geocachers and promoted on the primary geocaching Web site (www.geocaching.com) that is designed to clean up areas where trash has accumulated. Geocachers promote an event, at which they meet and pick up trash, disposing of it responsibly.

cardinal points—North, east, south, and west points on a compass, or 0/360, 90, 180, and 270 degrees, respectively.

cardiorespiratory fitness—The ability of the body to perform large-muscle, dynamic exercise for a prolonged time.

Cartesian coordinates—The system of mathematical coordinates used to locate a point relative to a fixed reference along two axes, first proposed by René Descartes.

coniferous—A type of tree that has needles and stays green year round.

deciduous—A type of tree that sheds its leaves each year (e.g., maple, oak, elm).

declination—The difference between true north and magnetic north; declination varies at different locations across the planet. The value of declination at any point represented on a map is normally contained in the map's legend.

earthcache—A geocache with special geological features such as a rock formation, glacier, highest point east of the Mississippi, continental divide, karst formation, and so on.

EasyGPS—A computer software program that facilitates loading coordinates onto a GPS unit.

e-punch—An electronic punch used in the sport of orienteering as an alternative to the traditional mechanical punches made of bright orange or red plastic.

event cache—A geocaching event with a predetermined goal such as gathering with fellow cachers to eat a meal and discuss the finer points of caching or picking up litter at a site.

exercise frequency—The number of days recommended for exercise. For cardiorespiratory fitness, daily exercise is recommended. For muscular strength and bone strength, three days of exercise a week are recommended.

exercise intensity—How hard a person exercises, as measured by heart rate, breathing rate, or degree of exertion. For cardiorespiratory fitness, moderate and vigorous exercise is recommended.

exercise time—How long a person exercises, often measured in minutes of exercise. It is recommended that children perform 60 minutes of exercise daily.

geocache—Often abbreviated to *cache*, a geocache is a hidden container housing a logbook and trinkets that is registered on geocaching.com. Although a geocache can take many forms, this original form is what most people term a *geocache*. Also referred to as a *traditional cache*, distinguishing it from other forms of geocache that have evolved since geocaching began.

geocachers—People that look for geocaches; often abbreviated to *cachers*.

geocoins—Coins with unique tracking numbers that are created for geocachers to leave as a trinket in a geocache. The unique tracking number allows a person to track the path of the coin as it travels from geocache to geocache.

Global Positioning System (GPS)—An electronic device that triangulates its position on earth relative to orbiting satellites.

grandfathered caches—Geocaches that were popular at various times but are no longer supported by geocaching.com. They include the locationless cache, the Webcam cache, and the virtual cache.

grid north—A navigational term referring to grid lines drawn on a map to indicate the direction of north.

Groundspeak—The company that runs the geocaching.com Web site, whose mission is to inspire outdoor play using location-based technology.

intercardinal points—The four directions between the cardinal points: northeast, southeast, northwest, and southwest.

latitude—A numeric representation of location on the earth relative to imaginary lines that encircle the earth parallel to the equator. In combination with lines of longitude, they form an imaginary grid over the earth's surface. The equator is 0° latitude.

letterbox hybrid—A mixture of letterboxing and geocaching. The container contains the signature stamp that stays in the box (just as it does for letterboxing), but it also conforms to the geocaching guidelines by including a logbook and being located by GPS.

letterboxing—An activity similar to geocaching in which people hunt for rubber inking stamps left by previous letterboxers.

locationless cache—The locationless cache has now become known as a *waymark* (or sometimes as a *reverse cache*). Participants look for items (waymarks) that fit a theme and post the coordinates of those items as proof of having found them. For example, a locationless cache (or waymark) might set the challenge of finding statues containing or depicting animals.

longitude—A numeric representation of location on the earth relative to imaginary lines that encircle the earth perpendicular to the equator. In combination with lines of latitude, they form an imaginary grid over the earth's surface. The line of 0° longitude runs through the Royal Observatory at Greenwich, England.

magnetic north—The point to which compasses are drawn by the earth's magnetic field.

meetings—A time for fellow cachers to gather and share ideas, discuss a variety of topics, and meet other local cachers. This is a time for cachers to socialize and have fun.

mega-event caches—Very large event caches, attended by at least 500 people. They are typically annual events and attract geocachers from all over the world.

microcaches—Traditional geocaches that are comprised of a small container with little or no room for anything but a log. An empty 35mm film canister is a typical microcache container.

minicaches—Small geocaches that are larger than microcaches but smaller than an average traditional geocache.

muggles—People who are not geocachers and do not know about geocaching.

multistage cache—A geocache that requires cachers to locate multiple coordinates before reaching the final coordinates.

muscular strength—The muscles' ability to generate force.

mystery cache—Similar to a multistage cache in that it may involve visiting multiple locations and it has a strong problem-solving component. The difference is that the problem solving becomes the central component. A typical example would be that a story provides clues that make sense only when a person stands at the location. Also known as *puzzle cache*.

National Geodetic Survey (NGS)—A U.S. federal agency that defines and manages a national coordinate system used in mapping, charting, and other scientific and engineering applications.

orienteering—A sport that tests navigational skills in participants who race from point to point along a predetermined course.

radio frequency identification (RFID)—A tag that emits a unique identification signal that can be tracked using radio waves.

rogaining—Long-distance orienteering; rogaining controls are often less hidden—in fact, the controls are sometimes highly visible checkpoints—but the principle of searching with a map and coordinates clearly embraces a significant component of geocaching.

selective availability (SA)—Before 2000, GPS signals were intentionally degraded through a process known as selective availability (SA), which had been in place to restrict the accurate use of GPS to the U.S. military.

topographic map—A map that is printed according to scale with geological features such as declination, rivers, roads, streams, hiking trails, and so on.

trackable item—An item that carries a unique code that can be tracked as the item moves between multiple geocaches (e.g., a travel bug).

traditional cache—The first kind of cache to emerge, it's the most common and the most easily recognized type of geocache. A traditional cache is some form of waterproof container that is used to store a logbook, a pen or pencil, and a few trinkets for people to exchange. The size and type of container used for these caches vary greatly.

travel bug—A user-created and -defined trackable item that moves between geocache sites.

type of exercise—The kind of exercise being performed. For cardiorespiratory fitness, the exercise must be aerobic and use large muscles of the body. For muscular strength, body weight exercises, resistance band exercises, and hand weight exercises are recommended. For bone strength, activities that involve foot impact with the ground are recommended.

virtual cache—A variation of the locationless cache. For the virtual cache, the waymark is not a specific item but rather the location itself.

waymarking—A scavenger hunt for interesting locations around the world. Participants locate and log locations before sharing their find through a Web site, the largest of which is www.waymarking.com. Waymarking is sometimes referred to as *reverse geocaching*.

Webcam cache—A grandfathered cache that is popular among technology-oriented geocachers. The goal is to appear on one of the many Webcams that are live-streamed over the Internet. For a Webcam cache to work, the would-be geocacher first finds a Webcam that is viewable by the general public. The geocacher then lines up an accomplice to take a screenshot of that Webcam while the geocacher is standing in the camera's gaze. Although no longer supported by geocaching.com, it remains an interesting activity for many people.

Wherigo—An activity that combines geocaching with adventure gaming. Wherigo enthusiasts use a programming language called Lua to build "cartridges" or adventures for people to follow by visiting the locations using their GPS. A simple Wherigo cartridge might involve a guided tour of a particular area. A more complex cartridge might involve interactive games in which game characters respond differently according to the location of the GPS. Wherigo is hosted at its own Web site (www.wherigo.com).

World Geodetic System (WGS84)—A standardized system use in cartography, geodesy, and navigation. The latest revision of the system was made in 1984, giving rise to the abbreviation for this system (WGS84).

REFERENCES AND RESOURCES

AAA Fuel Gauge Report: www.fuelgaugereport.com

ACME Mapper: http://mapper.acme.com

ACSM. (2006). *ACSM's guidelines for exercise testing and prescription* (7th ed.). Philadelphia: Lippincott, Williams & Wilkins.

Arborday.org Tree Guide: www.arborday.org/trees/treeguide/

Boys and Girls Clubs of America. (2009). Mission. www.bgca.org/whoweare/mission.asp.

Burns, B., & Burns, M. (2004). *Wilderness navigation: Finding your way using map, compass, altimeter, and GPS.* Seattle: The Mountaineers Books.

Compass Store: www.thecompassstore.com

Cone, T.P., Werner, P., & Cone, S.L. (2009). *Interdisciplinary elementary physical education* (2nd ed.). Champaign, IL: Human Kinetics.

Earthcache: www.earthcache.org

Educaching: www.educaching.com

Education Place: Outline Maps (United States): www.eduplace.com/ss/maps/usa.html

Education Place: Outline Maps (U.S. states): www.eduplace.com/ss/maps/states.html

Gega, P. (1994). *Concepts and experiences in elementary school science.* Columbus, OH: Merrill.

Geocaching: www.geocaching.com

Google Earth: http://earth.google.com

Granstrom, C. (2006). They live and breathe letterboxing. www.letterboxing.org/Smithsonian.html.

Hubbard, J. (2008). *Educaching GPS based curriculum for teachers: Grades 4-8.* Maumee, OH: SDG Creations, Inc.

iTouchMap: http://itouchmap.com/latlong.html

Jacobson, C. (2007). *Basic essentials: Map and compass.* Guilford, CT: Falcon Guide.

Kjellstrom, B. (2009). *Be an expert with map and compass.* New York: John Wiley & Sons.

Letterboxing North America: www.letterboxing.org

Library of Congress Classification Outline: www.loc.gov/catdir/cpso/lcco/

Lions Club International. (2009). Main page. www.lionsclubs.org/EN/.

Lynn, S.K., Castelli, D.M., Werner, P., & Cone, S.L. (2007). *Seminar in physical education: From student teaching to teaching students.* Champaign, IL: Human Kinetics.

Magyari, P., & Meyer, R. (2009). Geocaching: Utilizing technology to increase physical activity on campus. Presentation at Southeast Chapter of the American College of Sports Medicine (February).

MapQuest: www.mapquest.com

Math Warehouse: www.mathwarehouse.com

McNamara, J. (2004). *GPS for dummies.* Hoboken, NJ: Wiley.

Measuring Physical Activity Intensity: www.cdc.gov/physicalactivity/everyone/measuring/index.html

Mother Road: Historic Route 66: www.historic66.com

National Association for Sport and Physical Education. (2004). *Moving into the future: National standards for physical education* (2nd ed.). Boston: McGraw-Hill.

National Council for Social Studies. (1994). *Curriculum standards for social studies.* Silver Spring, MD: Author.

National Council of Teachers of English and International Reading Association. (1996). *National standards for the English language arts.* Newark, DE: Author.

National Council of Teachers of Mathematics. (2000). *Principles and standards for school mathematics.* Reston, VA: Author.

National Park Service: Teaching With Historic Places: www.nps.gov/history/NR/twhp/descrip.htm

National Research Council. (1996). *National science education standards.* Washington, DC: National Academies Press.

OCLC: Dewey Decimal Classification Summaries: www.oclc.org/us/en/dewey/support/default.htm

Palk, J.M. (2008, December 30). Geocaching scavenger hunt goes through Md. *The Frederick News-Post* (Frederick, MD).

Petrides, G.A., Petrides, O., & Peterson, R.T. (1998). *A field guide to western trees.* Boston: Houghton Mifflin.

Petrides, G.A., Wehr, J., & Peterson, R.T. (1998). *A field guide to eastern trees.* Boston: Houghton Mifflin.

Powers, S., & Howley, E. (2007). *Exercise physiology: Theory and application to fitness and performance* (6th ed.). New York: McGraw-Hill.

Print Free Graph Paper: www.printfreegraphpaper.com

Rotary International. (2010). About us. www.rotary.org/en/aboutus/rotaryinternational/Pages/ridefault.aspx.

Route 66: The Great American Highway: www.theroadwanderer.net/route66.htm

Shape Up America! (2009). 10,000 steps. www.shapeup.org/shape/steps.php.

ThinkQuest: Chromosomes and Cell Division: http://library.thinkquest.org/20465/mitosis.html

ThinkQuest: "Do We" Really Know Dewey?: http://library.thinkquest.org/5002/

Tudor-Locke, C., Pangrazi, R.P., Corbin, C.B., Rutherford, W.J., Vincent, S.D., Raustorp, A., et al. (2004). BMI-referenced standards for recommended pedometer-determined steps/day in children. *Preventive Medicine, 38,* 857-864.

University of Wisconsin-Stevens Point. (2001). *LEAF: The Wisconsin K-12 Forestry Education Program.* Stevens Point, WI: Author.

U.S. Department of Health & Human Services. (2008). Physical activity guidelines for Americans (chapter 3: Active children and adolescents). www.health.gov/PAGuidelines/guidelines/chapter3.aspx.

Virginia Tech Forest Biology and Dendrology: www.fw.vt.edu/dendro

Waymarking: www.waymarking.com

Wherigo: www.wherigo.com

ABOUT THE AUTHORS

J. Kevin Taylor, PhD, is a professor in the kinesiology department at Cal Poly San Luis Obispo in California. He has trained physical education teachers and taught outdoor education since 1994 and has made more than 50 professional presentations at national, state, and regional conferences. In his leisure time, he enjoys being with and playing with his family, playing soccer, and riding his bicycle.

DuAnn E. Kremer, PhD, HFS, is an associate professor of exercise physiology at Lynchburg College in Virginia. One of her areas of interest is in motivating people to increase their physical activity. She is a member of AAHPERD and ACSM and has made numerous national geocaching presentations. She is an experienced geocacher, with more than 300 finds, and she also enjoys kayaking, hiking, and mountain biking in her spare time.

Katherine Pebworth, PhD, is an associate professor and department chair of physical education and kinesiology at Lincoln Memorial University (LMU) in Harrogate, Tennessee. She is a lifetime member of AAHPERD and has made numerous geocaching presentations at the state, district, and national levels. She enjoys hiking, geocaching, and watching sports at LMU.

Peter Werner, PED, is a distinguished professor emeritus at the University of South Carolina in Columbia. He has written three related books on interdisciplinary learning and edited the film series for the American Master Teacher Program. He is a lifetime member of AAHPERD and served as chair of the Editorial Review Board for Strategies in 2007-08 and as senior editor of *Teaching Elementary Physical Education* from 2000 to 2003. He has made numerous geocaching presentations at all levels, takes to the waters as a whitewater canoeist, and enjoys broom making and fly fishing.